CERTIFIED
SPECIALIST
OF WINE

INTRODUCTION TO THE CERTIFIED SPECIALIST OF WINE WORKBOOK

The Certified Specialist of Wine (CSW) credential represents the Society of Wine Educators' recognition that the holder has attained a broad base of knowledge about wine, equivalent to a midlevel wine professional. The CSW Study Guide, published by the Society of Wine Educators, is the approved study tool for the CSW and covers the depth of information needed to successfully pass the CSW Certification Exam.

This workbook is intended to accompany the 2020 version of the CSW Study Guide. Used properly, this workbook should be an invaluable tool for all CSW candidates.

The chapters in this workbook follow the chapters in the CSW Study Guide. We recommend that you first read and study a chapter in the Study Guide, and then complete the exercises in the workbook. These exercises are intended to both assess your comprehension and to increase your memory retention of the subject matter. The exercises are organized according to the major topic headings within the Study Guide itself.

After you read each chapter, try to answer the questions without consulting the Study Guide, and then check your answers by using the online answer key. Each chapter's exercises include a short "checkpoint" quiz intended to test your knowledge after you have completed your study of the chapter.

Keep in mind that while the exercises in this workbook cover much of the information found in our Study Guide, any information found in the Study Guide is considered fair game to be used as the basis for questions found on our Certified Specialist of Wine Exam.

ANSWER KEY

The answer key for this workbook is available online at SWE's blog site at http://winewitandwisdomswe.com/study-guide-updates/csw-updates/csw-workbook-answer-key/.

A NOTE ON MAPS

The maps in the CSW Study Guide are available electronically on the SWE blog, *Wine, Wit, and Wisdom*. The URL is: http://winewitandwisdomswe.com/swe-wine-maps/. The maps are considered an integral part of the material in the Study Guide and form the basis for many of the exercises contained within this workbook.

This publication is intended to provide accurate information in regard to the subject matter covered; however, facts and figures regarding numbers of appellations, relative rankings of countries, and wine laws are all liable to change over time. Please contact the Society of Wine Educators if you have any questions or comments about the contents of this workbook or the accompanying CSW Study Guide.

The answer key for this workbook is available online at SWE's blog site at http://winewitandwisdomswe.com/study-guide-updates/csw-updates/csw-workbook-answer-key/

Printed in the United States of America

RESOURCES FOR CSW CANDIDATES

The Society of Wine Educators offers many resources for CSW students and exam candidates, including the following:

Webinars: Monthly SWEbinars, available at no charge and to the public, covering CSW- and CSS-related topics. For more information, including the schedule, see the SWEbinar webpage at SWE's blog, http://winewitandwisdomswe.com/.

Online Prep Classes: Several times a year, SWE offers guided online prep classes covering the CSW Study Guide. These classes are offered free of charge for professional members of SWE who hold a current CSW Exam attendance credit. For more information, contact Jane Nickles at jnickles@societyofwineeducators.org.

Study Guide Updates: To assist all members of the adult beverage industry so that they may keep up with the ever-changing world of wine and spirits, SWE maintains "Study Guide Updates" pages for both the CSW and CSS Study Guides. Any changes that occur in the regulatory landscape, or elsewhere, that affect the information in the Study Guides will be updated on these pages. To access our Study Guide Updates page, see http://winewitandwisdomswe.com/study-guide-updates/.

eBook: Our CSW Study Guide is available as an eBook on both Amazon and iTunes.

CSW Exams: The CSW Exam consists of 100 multiple-choice questions, with all question content drawn exclusively from the CSW Study Guide. Candidates are provided with one (1) hour in which to complete the exam. CSW Exams are offered most days of the year throughout the world, by appointment, at Pearson VUE Testing Centers. To find a Pearson VUE Center near you, use the search function on SWE's landing page at the Pearson VUE website: http://www.pearsonvue.com/societyofwineeducators/.

Exams based on the 2020 version of the CSW Study Guide will be available at Pearson VUE Testing Centers through December 30, 2022.

A FINAL NOTE

We hope that this workbook is useful to you in your studies, and we wish you the best of luck as you prepare to sit for the Certification Exam. Hopefully, we will soon be able to welcome you into the ranks of Certified Specialists of Wine!

An Educational
Resource Published
by the Society of
Wine Educators

SOCIETY
of WINE
EDUCATORS

CERTIFIED
SPECIALIST
OF WINE

WORKBOOK
To Accompany the
2020 CSW Study Guide

TABLE OF CONTENTS

SOCIETY
of WINE
EDUCATORS

WINE
DEFINED

UNIT ONE

WINE COMPOSITION AND CHEMISTRY

CHAPTER ONE

LEARNING OBJECTIVES

After studying this chapter, the candidate should be able to:

- Recognize the main categories of chemical compounds in wine.
- Identify the approximate concentrations of the major components of wine.
- Describe the specific types of alcohols, acids, and sugars that are most prominent in wine.
- Discuss the types of phenolic compounds that are important in wine.

EXERCISE 1: WINE COMPONENTS: MATCHING

Match each of the following terms with its appropriate definition. Each term will be used only once.

Water	Glycerol	Tartaric acid	Citric acid	Acetic acid
Ethyl alcohol	Legs	Malic acid	Lactic acid	Succinic acid

1. _Tartaric Acid_ — The most prevalent of the acids found in grapes and wine

2. _Water_ — The component that makes up 80–90% of the volume of most wines

3. _Legs_ — Slow-moving "tears" that may appear in a wine glass after the wine is swirled

4. _Citric Acid_ — Has little or no sensory impact on the majority of quality wines

5. _Ethyl Alcohol_ — The component that makes up 10–15% of the volume of most wines

6. _Glycerol_ — A type of secondary alcohol

7. _Malic Acid_ — A sharp-tasting acid often associated with green apples

8. _Lactic Acid_ — An acid produced via the conversion of malic acid

9. _Acetic Acid_ — An acid with a slightly bitter, slightly salty flavor

10. _Succinic Acid_ — The acid found in most types of vinegar

Please fill in the blanks or give a short answer for the following statements or questions.

1. Of the six main acids found in wine, list those that are typically found in unfermented grapes.

   Tartaric, Malic, Citric, Succinic

2. Of the acids typically found in grapes, which are found in very small quantities?

   Succinic, Citric

3. Which acid is known to cause deposits known as wine diamonds?

   Tartaric Acids

4. What is the name of the winemaking process that, in addition to changing a wine's acid components, often provides wines with a creamy texture and a buttery aroma?

   Malolactic Fermentation

5. What measurement is used to define the volume of all the acids present in a wine?

   TA - Total Acidity

6. What does pH measure?

   Chemical Strengths of Acids

7. What is a typical pH measurement of a highly acidic wine?

   _2.9_

8. What pH measurement would you expect to find in a low-acid wine?

   _3.9_

9. What are the two main fermentable sugars found in wine grapes?

   Glucose & Fructose

10. What term is used to describe a wine that does not contain any detectable sugar?

    Dry

EXERCISE 3: PHENOLIC COMPOUNDS AND OTHER COMPONENTS: MATCHING

Match each of the following terms with its appropriate definition. Each term will be used only once.

Anthocyanins   Sulfur   Resveratrol   Acetaldehyde
Vanillin   Aldehydes   Sediment   Carbon dioxide
Esters   Tannins   Ethyl acetate   Flavonols

1. _Flavonols_   Yellow pigments found in white wine

2. _Vanillin_   An aromatic compound found in oak barrels

3. _Resveratrol_   A compound found in wine believed to be beneficial to human health

4. _Ethyl Acetate_   One of the most common esters found in wine

5. _Acetaldehyde_   The specific component that gives fino Sherries their distinctive aroma

6. _Anthocyanins_   The compounds that give red wine its red, blue, or purple hue

7. _Tannins_   Bitter compounds found in the skins, seeds, and stems of grapes

8. _Esters_   Molecules that result from the joining of an acid and an alcohol

9. _Sediment_   Matter sometimes formed as a result of polymerization

10. _Sulfur_   A preservative widely used in winemaking

11. _Aldehydes_   Oxidized alcohols formed when wine is exposed to air

12. _Carbon Dioxide_   Promotes the release of the wine's aromatic compounds

Mark each of the following statements as true or false.

1. _False_ Red wines that are highly acidic tend to appear more blue in color, whereas low-acid red wines appear more red.

2. _True_ Tannins can create a textural, drying sensation on the palate.

3. _True_ Madeira is an example of a wine that is produced in such a way that oxidation is encouraged and expected.

4. _True_ Flavonols increase in white grapes with increased exposure to sunlight.

5. _False_ The aromatic compound vanillin, found in vanilla beans, is not found anywhere else in nature.

6. _False_ The phenolic compounds of a grape are concentrated primarily in its skin and seeds.

7. _True_ Wines may become oxidized after being exposed to heat.

8. _False_ It is common for winemakers to encourage the oxidation of white wines such as Chenin Blanc and Riesling by maximizing air exposure during the preliminary stages of fermentation and aging.

9. _False_ Ethyl acetate imparts an aroma similar to nail polish remover or glue at very low concentrations, whereas at higher concentrations it tends to smell of dried rose petals or perfume.

10. _True_ Esters represent the largest group of odiferous compounds found in wine.

11. _False_ Wines with greater than 2 ppm of sulfur dioxide are required to display the "Contains Sulfites" warning on the label.

12. _False_ Normal fermentation does not produce enough carbon dioxide to make a difference in the flavor profile of a typical table wine.

1. Which of the following is the most prevalent type of acid found in both vinifera grapes and wine?
   a. Acetic acid
   b. Citric acid
   c. Tartaric acid
   d. Malic acid

2. Which of the following phenolic compounds is responsible for the bitter taste and drying textural sensation found in many red wines?
   a. Vanillin
   b. Tannin
   c. Anthocyanins
   d. Sulfites

3. Which of the following is a type of molecule that results from the joining of an acid and an alcohol?
   a. Aldehydes
   b. Sulfites
   c. Flavonols
   d. Esters

4. What is the typical pH range found in table wines?
   a. 2.5 to 3.5
   b. 1.9 to 2.7
   c. 2.9 to 3.9
   d. 3.9 to 4.7

5. What is a wine diamond?
   a. A small particle created via the crystallization of tartaric acid
   b. Tannic sediment created via polymerization
   c. A by-product of malolactic fermentation that can create a buttery aroma
   d. A by-product of the fermentation of fructose

6. What is methyl alcohol?
   a. The primary alcohol component of wine
   b. A by-product of polymerization
   c. A secondary alcohol produced via fermentation
   d. A phenolic compound that provides a citrus-fruit flavor in many wines

7. In the United States, wine with more than 10 ppm of this compound must have a warning label.
   a. Dissolved gasses
   b. Sulfites
   c. Esters
   d. Acetic acid

8. Which of the following compounds gives red wines their red, blue, or purple hues?
   a. Anthocyanins
   b. Tannins
   c. Aldehydes
   d. Resveratrol

9. Which of the following acids, created in small amounts during typical fermentation, is found in many types of vinegar?
   a. Succinic acid
   b. Malic acid
   c. Citric acid
   d. Acetic acid

10. Which of the following compounds could cause a wine to have slow, thick tears?
    a. Malic acid
    b. Flavonols
    c. Alcohol
    d. Aldehydes

WINE FAULTS

CHAPTER TWO

LEARNING OBJECTIVES

After studying this chapter, the candidate should be able to:

- Recall the main terminology associated with wine faults.
- Describe the source and effect of cork taint.
- Discuss the impact of sulfur compounds on wine.
- Recognize which odors are acceptable and under which conditions.

EXERCISE 1: WINE FAULTS: MATCHING

Match each of the following wine faults and off-odors with its most likely source. Terms may be used more than once.

Sulfur compounds
Bacteria
Yeast
Mold
Oxidation

1. _Bacteria_   Acetic acid

2. _Yeast_   Pronounced odor of lees

3. _Oxidation_   Acetaldehyde

4. _Sulfur_   Mercaptan

5. _~~Sulfur~~ Mold_   Cork taint

6. _Bacteria_   Ascensence

7. _Bacteria_   Butyric acid

8. _Oxidation_   Browning

9. _Yeast_   Brettanomyces

10. _Bacteria_   Geranium

Please fill in the blanks or give a short answer for the following statements or questions.

1. What compound is the root cause of cork taint?

   TNA

2. What specific terms can be used to describe the aroma of a "corked" wine?

   Musty, moldy, Dank Basement

3. What substance can cause a wine to smell like rancid butter?

   Butyric Acid

4. What faulty wine aroma can be caused by incomplete malolactic fermentation?

   Sauerkraut, goat

5. What is the term used to describe a wine that has a cooked or baked odor?

   Madeirized

6. What wine fault is typically caused by high amounts of both acetic acid and ethyl acetate?

   Ascensence

7. What specific terms can be used to describe a wine with an excess of Brett?

   Sweaty, horsey, Band-aid, Medicinal

8. What substance can cause a wine to smell like onions or garlic?

   Mer Ethyl Mercaptan

9. What aroma can be caused by an excess of ethyl acetate?

   Fingernail Polish remover, glue

10. What wine fault can be described as having the aroma of burnt matches?

    Sulfur Dioxide, Reduction

11. What wine fault is often described as similar to rotten eggs?

    Hydrogen Sulfide, Reduction

12. What off-odor is caused by acetic acid?

    Vinegar

1. Which of the following wine odors can occur as a result of prolonged contact with dead yeast cells?
   a. Ethyl acetate
   b. Leesy
   c. Geranium
   d. Onions or garlic

2. Which of the following wine faults can occur as a result of sulfur compounds?
   a. Butyric acid
   b. Oxidation
   c. Lactic acid
   d. Mercaptan

3. Which of the following wine faults can occur as a result of an excess of Brettanomyces?
   a. Sweaty or horsy odor
   b. Citric or lemony aroma
   c. Rancid butter or spoiled cheese odor
   d. Vinegar odor

4. Which of the following compounds is responsible for cork taint?
   a. Acetic acid
   b. 2,4,6-Trichloroanisole
   c. Butyric acid
   d. Hydrogen sulfide

5. What aroma can be caused by an excess of ethyl acetate?
   a. Geranium
   b. Wet cardboard
   c. Vinegar
   d. Fingernail polish remover

6. What faulty wine aroma can be caused by incomplete malolactic fermentation?
   a. Wet cardboard
   b. Oxidized
   c. Geranium
   d. Brett

7. TCA is noticeable at very _____ concentrations, with most people able to detect it at the level of _____
   a. Low, 2 to 7 parts per trillion
   b. Low, 100 to 120 parts per trillion
   c. High, 2,000 to 5,000 parts per million
   d. High, 10,000 to 20,000 parts per million

8. What wine fault can lead to the aroma of rotten eggs?
   a. Brettanomyces
   b. Hydrogen sulfide
   c. Ethyl acetate
   d. Mercaptan

CERTIFIED SPECIALIST OF WINE

VITICULTURE AND ENOLOGY

UNIT TWO

GRAPE VARIETIES

CHAPTER THREE

LEARNING OBJECTIVES

After studying this chapter, the candidate should be able to:

- State the differences between *Vitis vinifera* and other vine species.
- Discuss hybrids, crossings, and clones.
- Describe the primary characteristics of the classic international white grape varieties.
- Describe the primary characteristics of the classic international red grape varieties.

EXERCISE 1: GRAPEVINE SPECIES AND VARIETIES: MATCHING

Match each of the following terms with its appropriate definition. Terms may be used more than once.

Cross	Variety	Autochthonous	Species	Hybrid
Mutation	Seyval Blanc	Cabernet Sauvignon	International	Clone

1. _____ An example of a hybrid grape

2. _____ An example of a grape that was produced via a crossing

3. _____ A scientific grouping of plants or animals that are genetically similar and can produce viable offspring via sexual reproduction

4. _____ The name for the category of grapes that result from the sexual reproduction between a *Vitis vinifera* grape and a *Vitis labrusca* grape

5. _____ Term used for the offspring of sexual reproduction between two *Vitis vinifera* grapes

6. _____ Term used for a subspecies of *Vitis vinifera*

7. _____ Term used for indigenous grapes that are the result of natural cross-breeding or natural mutation in a specific area

8. _____ A term used for grape varieties that have been found to thrive in a wide range of environments

9. _____ Term used for an asexually reproduced vine that has modified itself to be slightly different from its parent

10. _____ A grape variety derived from a vine that has different characteristics from its parents via imperfect reproduction of its cells as it grows

11. _____ A type of grape variety that often has a number assigned to it

12. _____ A grape that is a result of the sexual reproduction of grapes from two different but closely related species

Match each of the following wine-producing areas with the grape variety from the list with which it is most closely associated.

Chardonnay	Pinot Gris	Semillon	Ugni Blanc
Chenin Blanc	Riesling	Viognier	Torrontés
Muscat	Sauvignon Blanc	Albariño	Furmint

1. _____ Argentina

2. _____ Northern Rhône

3. _____ Hunter Valley (Australia)

4. _____ Burgundy

5. _____ Rutherglen (Australia)

6. _____ Cognac

7. _____ Sancerre

8. _____ Eden Valley (Australia)

9. _____ Northeast Italy; Oregon (United States)

10. _____ Vouvray

11. _____ Spain

12. _____ Hungary

13. _____ Pouilly-Fumé

14. _____ Savennières

EXERCISE 3: RED GRAPE VARIETIES: TRUE OR FALSE

Mark each of the following statements as true or false.

1. _____ Tempranillo is the sole ingredient in many of the red wines of Piedmont, Italy.

2. _____ Zinfandel is known for producing robust red wines as well as off-dry blush wines.

3. _____ Merlot ripens late, and Cabernet Sauvignon ripens early.

4. _____ Cabernet Sauvignon, Cabernet Franc, and Merlot are all grown in Bordeaux.

5. _____ Cabernet Sauvignon is the most widely planted quality red grape in the world.

6. _____ The Chinon AOC produces a red wine based on Cabernet Franc.

7. _____ Merlot is known as Spätburgunder in Germany.

8. _____ Grenache is grown in the Spanish region of Priorat.

9. _____ In the United States, *Zinfandel* is a legally approved synonym for *Primitivo*.

10. _____ Pinot Noir is grown in the Champagne region of France.

11. _____ Malbec is referred to as Cannonau on the island of Sardinia.

12. _____ Sangiovese is the main grape variety used in the wines of the Chianti DOCG.

13. _____ Tempranillo is not grown in Portugal.

14. _____ Syrah and Shiraz are actually the same grape variety.

15. _____ Barolo is made from 100% Nebbiolo.

Name the grape varieties described by the following statements.

1. _____ Italian variety known to have aromas of tar and roses

2. _____ The main variety in "the black wine of Cahors"

3. _____ White grape variety that can be coaxed into a wide variety of styles, including a "California style" that often has aromas of butterscotch, vanilla, and tropical fruit

4. _____ Also known as Pinot Grigio

5. _____ Red grape grown in Burgundy, New Zealand, and Oregon

6. _____ Italian variety known to have a characteristic sour cherry and orange peel flavor profile

7. _____ The leading red grape of Spain

8. _____ Also known as Ugni Blanc

9. _____ One of the most aromatic white grape varieties, known for aromas of perfume, flowers, spice, lychee, and rose

10. _____ Red grape variety often used in a blend along with Grenache and Mourvèdre

11. _____ Widely planted white grape variety known for aromas of musk, honey, apricot, table grapes, and orange blossom

12. _____ Red grape variety that is native to France, but that has achieved renown in Argentina

13. _____ White grape that often shows gasoline- or petrol-like aromas

14. _____ Also known as Weissburgunder

15. _____ The most widely planted grape in South Africa

1. Which of the following is true concerning Seyval Blanc and Baco Noir grapes?
   a. They are *Vitis labrusca* varieties.
   b. They are *Vitis vinifera* varieties.
   c. They are hybrids.
   d. They are clones.

2. The term *vinifera* refers to which of the following categories?
   a. A grapevine species
   b. A grapevine variety
   c. A grapevine family
   d. A grapevine genus

3. Which of the following grapes is primarily grown in Piedmont, Italy?
   a. Cabernet Sauvignon
   b. Chenin Blanc
   c. Sauvignon Blanc
   d. Nebbiolo

4. Which of the following grapes is also known as Grauburgunder?
   a. Pinot Noir
   b. Pinot Gris
   c. Chardonnay
   d. Pinot Blanc

5. Which of the following grape varieties is known for showing fruity, mineral, and petrol-like aromas?
   a. Chenin Blanc
   b. Viognier
   c. Sauvignon Blanc
   d. Riesling

6. Which of the following wines is made from a majority of Cabernet Franc?
   a. Left Bank Bordeaux
   b. Morgon
   c. Chinon
   d. Vouvray

7. Which of the following wines is most likely made from a majority of Merlot?
   a. Right Bank Bordeaux
   b. Left Bank Bordeaux
   c. Rioja
   d. Chianti

8. Which of the following is the leading red grape of Australia?
   a. Merlot
   b. Cabernet Sauvignon
   c. Syrah
   d. Zinfandel

9. The Concord grape is a member of which of the following groups?
   a. *Vitis vinifera*
   b. *Vitis labrusca*
   c. Grapevine species
   d. Hybrid grapes

10. Australia's Hunter Valley is best known for which of the following grape varieties?
    a. Semillon
    b. Sauvignon Blanc
    c. Torrontés
    d. Chenin Blanc

11. Chenin Blanc is the most widely grown grape variety in which of the following countries?
    a. France
    b. Spain
    c. Argentina
    d. South Africa

12. Which of the following grapes is native to France, but is now grown extensively in Argentina?
    a. Merlot
    b. Malbec
    c. Pinot Noir
    d. Zinfandel

13. Which of the following grapes is also known as Ugni Blanc?
    a. Chardonnay
    b. Chenin Blanc
    c. Trebbiano Toscano
    d. Sauvignon Blanc

14. Which of the following grapes is also sometimes referred to as Cannonau?
    a. Cabernet Sauvignon
    b. Merlot
    c. Malbec
    d. Grenache

15. Which of the following regions produces a well-known wine from the Malbec grape variety?
    a. Cahors
    b. Montalcino
    c. Priorat
    d. Morgon

VITICULTURE

CHAPTER FOUR

LEARNING OBJECTIVES

After studying this chapter, the candidate should be able to:

- Describe the physical structure of a grapevine.
- Explain the annual life cycle and metabolic processes of the vine.
- Identify the factors that affect the amount of sugar and acid in grapes.
- Recognize the elements that make up the concept of terroir.
- Recall the effects of vine diseases, pests, and botrytis.
- Understand how viticultural practices such as organic, biodynamic, and sustainable differ from those of mainstream viticulture and from each other.

EXERCISE 1: GROWTH CYCLE OF THE VINE: TIMELINE

Put the following stages of the annual growth cycle of the vine in chronological order, starting with winter dormancy and following through the year.

Berry set

Photosynthesis begins

Harvest

Bud break

Physiological maturity

Veraison

Shoot and leaf growth

Flowering

Weeping

1. Winter dormancy _____

2. _____

3. _____

4. _____

5. _____

6. _____

7. _____

8. _____

9. _____

10. _____

Name the metabolic processes described by the following statements.

1. _____   The process by which materials are moved from one part of the plant to another

2. _____   The process by which sunlight is converted into sugar

3. _____   The process by which water evaporates through openings on the underside of the leaves

4. _____   The process by which sugar is broken down and converted into biological energy

EXERCISE 3: VINE PESTS, PROBLEMS, AND DISEASES: MATCHING

Match each of the following vine maladies with its appropriate definition. Each term will be used only once.

| Oidium | Peronospora | Botrytis cinerea | Millerandage |
| Coulure | Pierce's disease | Phylloxera | Nematode |

1. _____   A problem that causes poor fruit set, also known as shatter

2. _____   A soil-based roundworm that has become more prevalent with the increased use of shallow-rooted rootstock

3. _____   A mold that is sometimes beneficial, also known as noble rot

4. _____   A fungal disease also known as powdery mildew

5. _____   A problem with abnormal fruit set that causes grape bunches to have a high proportion of small, seedless berries mixed in with normal, larger berries

6. _____   A fungal disease also known as downy mildew

7. _____   A bacterial disease spread by insects such as the glassy-winged sharpshooter

8. _____   A destructive louse that feeds off the roots of vinifera vines

Please fill in the blanks or give a short answer for the following statements or questions.

1. What is the difference between climate and weather?

_____

_____

_____

2. How much water do grapevines need on an annual basis?

_____

3. Explain why soils with low fertility are generally ideal for commercial vineyards.

_____

_____

_____

4. Put these four soil types in order, from smallest in particle size to largest: gravel, silt, clay, and sand.

_____

_____

5. Describe the potential climatic differences between a vineyard situated at a high elevation and one situated on a valley floor.

_____

_____

_____

6. Explain the effect that large bodies of water have on the climate of a nearby vineyard.

_____

_____

_____

Mark each of the following statements as true or false.

1. _____ In general, a lower latitude translates into a warmer climate.

2. _____ The Oechsle system of measuring grape ripeness is widely used in France.

3. _____ Photosynthesis slows, but does not stop, at night.

4. _____ The annual growth cycle of the vine is considered to begin each year with bud break, which starts once temperatures reach 65°F (18°C) in the spring.

5. _____ When producing dry table wines, the typical time from bud break to harvest is 140 to 160 days.

6. _____ Ideally, soil should enable the vine's roots to access water when needed, but also ensure that excess water is drained away.

7. _____ In the Northern Hemisphere, a vineyard on a slope that faces north gets the most sun.

8. _____ Regions with a continental climate generally experience hotter summers and colder winters than regions with a Mediterranean climate.

9. _____ The Guyot system of vine training does not require the use of a trellis or wires.

10. _____ A Mediterranean climate is considered to have too short a growing season in order for grapes to ripen on a regular basis.

11. _____ In general, sugar as measured by degrees Brix will convert to alcohol by a conversion factor of 55%.

12. _____ Photosynthesis tends to slow down at temperatures below 50°F/10°C.

13. _____ A refractometer is used to measure the amount of rainfall that penetrates the topsoil to a depth of 6 inches (15 centimeters).

14. _____ In a pergola system, overhead vines are trained up a tall support and allowed to spread out horizontally.

15. _____ In the United States, biodynamic viticulture is regulated by the US Department of Agriculture.

1. Which of the following statements is true concerning photosynthesis?
   a. Photosynthesis occurs most efficiently when the daytime temperature is over 90°F (32°C).
   b. Photosynthesis occurs most efficiently when the daytime temperature is under 50°F (10°C).
   c. Photosynthesis slows but does not completely shut down at night.
   d. Photosynthesis can only occur when the sun is shining.

2. In general, how much water do vines need on an annual basis?
   a. 5 to 10 inches (13–25 cm)
   b. 10 to 20 inches (25–51 cm)
   c. 20 to 30 inches (51–76 cm)
   d. 50 to 60 inches (127–152 cm)

3. Which of the following best describes the vine process of veraison?
   a. Tiny shoots start to emerge from nodes in the vine's branches, soon growing to full canopy.
   b. The grapes begin a sudden acceleration toward maturation and begin to take on color.
   c. Carbohydrate reserves stored the previous year are directed toward rapid leaf and shoot growth.
   d. The acid level of the grapes starts to rapidly increase, while sugar levels drop.

4. Which of the following are considered the ideal latitudes for commercial wine grape growing in both the Northern and Southern Hemispheres?
   a. Between 10 and 30 degrees
   b. Between 20 and 40 degrees
   c. Between 25 and 45 degrees
   d. Between 30 and 50 degrees

5. Which of the following vineyard diseases is easily spread by the glassy-winged sharpshooter?
   a. Phylloxera
   b. Powdery mildew
   c. Pierce's disease
   d. Oidium

6. Which of the following represents the correct progression of the life cycle of a grapevine?
   a. Bud break, shoot and leaf growth, flowering, berry set, veraison, harvest
   b. Bud break, berry set, flowering, shoot and leaf growth, harvest, veraison
   c. Bud break, shoot and leaf growth, flowering, berry set, harvest, veraison
   d. Bud break, flowering, shoot and leaf growth, berry set, veraison, harvest

7. Which of the following vine conditions is sometimes beneficial, and may be referred to as "noble rot"?
   a. Oidium
   b. Peronospora
   c. Botrytis
   d. Coulure

8. Which of the following is a vine metabolic process in which sugar is broken down and converted into biological energy?
   a. Respiration
   b. Transpiration
   c. Translocation
   d. Photosynthesis

9. Which of the following temperatures signals the beginning of bud break in the spring?
   a. 40°F (4.5°C)
   b. 50°F (10°C)
   c. 60°F (16°C)
   d. 70°F (21°C)

10. Which of the following soil types has the smallest particle size?
    a. Sand
    b. Clay
    c. Silt
    d. Rocks

FERMENTATION AND STILL WINE PRODUCTION

CHAPTER FIVE

LEARNING OBJECTIVES

After studying this chapter, the candidate should be able to:
- Recall the sequence of events that take place during the winemaking process.
- Recognize key terminology associated with fermentation and wine production.

- Understand the differences between red, white, and rosé winemaking.
- Describe the procedures for making sweet wines.
- Discuss what makes organic, biodynamic, and kosher wines different from other wines.

EXERCISE 1: WHITE WINE PRODUCTION: TIMELINE

Put the following stages of white wine production in typical chronological order, starting with the harvest and following through the winemaking process. Note that many of these techniques are optional and therefore not always used in the winemaking process.

Sur lie aging	Clarification	Pressing	Juice settling	Blending
Sorting	Cold stabilization	Bottling	Inoculation	
Crushing	Barrel aging	Must adjustments	Fermentation	

1. Harvest _____

2. _____

3. _____

4. _____

5. _____

6. _____

7. _____

8. _____

9. _____

10. _____

11. _____

12. _____

13. _____

14. _____

EXERCISE 2: RED WINE PRODUCTION: TIMELINE

Put the following stages of red wine production in typical chronological order, starting with the harvest and following through the winemaking process. Note that many of these techniques are optional and therefore not always used in the winemaking process.

Crushing/destemming
Clarification
Extended maceration
Barrel aging

Pressing
Bottling
Cold soak
Cap management

Inoculation
Fermentation
Blending

Must adjustments
Sorting

1. Harvest _____

2. _____

3. _____

4. _____

5. _____

6. _____

7. _____

8. _____

9. _____

10. _____

11. _____

12. _____

13. _____

14. _____

EXERCISE 3: FERMENTATION AND STILL WINE PRODUCTION: MATCHING

Match each of the following terms with its appropriate definition. Each term will be used only once.

Carbonic maceration	Free run	Chaptalization	Racking
Barrique	Pomace	Bâtonnage	Fining
Débourbage	Must	Diacetyl	Sur lie aging

1. _____ A standard size (60 gallon/225 liter) oak barrel

2. _____ Letting the newly-pressed juice settle for a day or two before fermentation is allowed to begin

3. _____ Adding sugar to the must before fermentation begins

4. _____ Allowing the wine to rest on the dead yeast cells after fermentation has completed

5. _____ The stirring up of the dead yeast cells back into the liquid

6. _____ Grape juice, or the mixture of grape juice, seeds, and skins, that will be fermented and transformed into wine

7. _____ A chemical by-product of malolactic fermentation that imparts a buttery aroma to wine

8. _____ An enzymatic fermentation that occurs in the absence of oxygen within whole, unbroken grapes

9. _____ Considered to be the highest-quality juice in the batch

10. _____ The cake of compressed grape skins and seeds that remains behind after the final pressing of the juice or wine

11. _____ The use of gravity to remove suspended matter in a batch of newly fermented wine

12. _____ A clarification technique that uses an inert material to attract and bind to unwanted materials

For each of the following wine production processes, determine whether they are likely to be used in the production of red, white, or rosé styles of wine. Place a check mark in the column of every wine type that is likely to use each process.

Process	Red?	White?	Rosé?
1. Saignée	☐	☐	☐
2. De-stemming	☐	☐	☐
3. Cap management	☐	☐	☐
4. Fermentation at 50°F (10°C)	☐	☐	☐
5. Malolactic fermentation	☐	☐	☐
6. Sulfur additions	☐	☐	☐
7. Barrel aging	☐	☐	☐
8. Fermentation at 95°F (32°C)	☐	☐	☐
9. Extended maceration	☐	☐	☐
10. Must adjustments	☐	☐	☐
11. Direct press	☐	☐	☐
12. Blending	☐	☐	☐

EXERCISE 5: WINEMAKING PRACTICES: TRUE OR FALSE

Mark each of the following statements as true or false.

1. _____ Sulfur can be added at many points during the winemaking process.

2. _____ A type of spirit called grappa is often made from the leftovers of wine production.

3. _____ Chaptalization is used to produce a wine with high levels of residual sugar.

4. _____ France and Canada are the two primary sources for oak barrels used in American wine production.

5. _____ Dessert wines are produced in the Sauternes region of France using grapes that have been affected by *Botrytis cinerea*.

6. _____ Italy's famous Amarone wine is made using grapes that have frozen naturally on the vine.

7. _____ Weissherbst is a type of German rosé.

8. _____ A mevushal wine is a kosher wine that is free from limitations on who may handle the wine once it leaves the winery.

9. _____ The direct press method of rosé production is used to create pink wines with a deep rosy hue.

10. _____ The Riesling grape variety is often used in the production of Eiswein.

11. _____ In the production of orange wines, juice from white grapes spends a period of time ranging from several days to several months macerating with the grape skins.

12. _____ Malolactic fermentation is used more often on red wines than white wines.

13. _____ Most of the yeasts used in winemaking are strains of *Saccharomyces cerevisiae*.

14. _____ According to the New World school of thought, terroir is considered to be paramount in wine production and winemakers should interfere as little as possible in the winemaking process.

15. _____ Malolactic fermentation is an optional winemaking process that converts malic acid into lactic acid, resulting in an overall softer, smoother wine.

1. Which of the following types of wine are most likely to be produced using the process of saignée?
   a. Orange wines and sweet white wines
   b. Deep red wines and light rosé
   c. Crisp, dry white wines and very pale rosé
   d. Blanc de blancs sparkling wines

2. Which of the following terms is used to refer to the process of allowing newly-pressed juice to settle for a day or two before fermentation is allowed to begin?
   a. Débourbage
   b. Chaptalization
   c. Bâtonnage
   d. Stabilization

3. What is chaptalization?
   a. Adjusting the juice for acid before fermentation begins
   b. The use of oak chips or wood tannin during primary fermentation
   c. Adding sugar to the juice in order to boost alcohol content in the finished wine
   d. Allowing the grape stems to be crushed into the juice in order to increase tannin content

4. Which of the following is a chemical by-product of malolactic fermentation that often imparts a buttery aroma to wine?
   a. Succinic acid
   b. Diacetyl
   c. Aldehyde
   d. Hydrogen sulfide

5. Which of the following terms is used for the cake of compressed grape skins and seeds that remains behind after the final pressing of the juice or wine?
   a. Must
   b. Pomace
   c. Lees
   d. Free run

6. Which of the following terms is used for the mixture of juice, skins, and seeds that will be fermented into wine?
   a. Pomace
   b. Must
   c. Brett
   d. Vin gris

7. Which of the following processes uses whole, uncrushed grape clusters?
   a. Malolactic fermentation
   b. Secondary fermentation
   c. Carbonic maceration
   d. Bâtonnage

8. Very pale rosé is often produced in Provence using which of the following methods?
   a. Mutage
   b. Carbonic maceration
   c. Direct press
   d. Malolactic fermentation

9. What is sur lie aging?
   a. Using an inert material such as gelatin or egg whites to help clarify the wine
   b. Chilling the wine to around 32°F/0°C in order to prevent the formation of tartrates
   c. Using a centrifuge to clarify the wine
   d. Allowing the newly-fermented wine to rest on the dead yeast cells for a period of time

10. The mass of grape solids and skins that rises to the top of the fermentation tank during red wine fermentation is known by which of the following terms?
    a. The cap
    b. Délestage
    c. Pomace
    d. Barrique

SPARKLING WINE PRODUCTION

LEARNING OBJECTIVES

After studying this chapter, the candidate should be able to:

- Describe how sparkling wines are produced.
- Identify which grape varieties are commonly used in sparkling wines.
- Recall the sequence of events that takes place during the traditional sparkling wine production process.

- Recognize the different style categories of sparkling wines.
- Recall the terminology relating to sparkling wines.

EXERCISE 1: SPARKLING WINE PRODUCTION: MATCHING

Match each of the following terms with its appropriate definition. Each term will be used only once.

Dégorgement	Assemblage	Autolysis	Cuve close
Prise de mousse	Sur lie	Pupitre	
Remuage	Liqueur de tirage	Liqueur d'expédition	

1. _____ Added to the cuvée in order to initiate the second fermentation

2. _____ Turning the bottles and gently shaking them in order to get the dead yeast cells collected near the cap

3. _____ Time spent aging the wine on the yeast lees

4. _____ A rack used to hold bottles of wine during the riddling process

5. _____ The creation of the blended wine that will undergo a second fermentation and be turned into a sparkling wine

6. _____ The second alcoholic fermentation

7. _____ The process wherein the yeast cells begin to decompose and release their flavors

8. _____ An addition added just after disgorging a bottle of sparkling wine; also known as the dosage

9. _____ The process in which the bottle is opened and the yeast extracted

10. _____ Another name for the Charmat Method of sparkling wine production

Place the names of the styles of sparkling wine, listed below, in order from driest to sweetest.

Sec   Doux   Brut nature   Brut
Extra dry   Extra brut   Demi-sec

Driest: 1. _____

               2. _____

               3. _____

               4. _____

               5. _____

               6. _____

Sweetest: 7. _____

Fill in the blanks with the appropriate term for the different sizes of traditional Champagne bottles.

1. _____ Equivalent to 2 standard bottles

2. _____ Equivalent to 4 standard bottles

3. _____ Equivalent to 6 standard bottles

4. _____ Equivalent to 8 standard bottles

5. _____ Equivalent to 12 standard bottles

6. _____ Equivalent to 16 standard bottles

7. _____ Equivalent to 20 standard bottles

Mark each of the following statements as true or false.

1. _____ The term *autolysis* is used to refer to the decomposition of yeast cells during the process of sur lie aging.

2. _____ The traditional Champagne press is a wide, flat basket press, and many of them are still in use today.

3. _____ The base wine that will be used in the production of Champagne is generally left very sweet.

4. _____ A blanc de blancs sparkling wine is produced using just red grape varieties.

5. _____ Most Cava is technically blanc de noirs.

6. _____ Moscato d'Asti is produced using the partial fermentation method.

7. _____ The Ancestral Method of sparkling wine production is sometimes referred to as the *Méthode Rurale*.

8. _____ The term "California Champagne" may be used on some California wine labels, but only if approved before March 10, 2012.

9. _____ Most "house style" sparkling wines are blanc de blancs, extra dry, and produced using the grapes of just one vintage.

10. _____ The second fermentation of a sparkling wine generally increases the alcohol content by one or two percentage points.

11. _____ The typical pressure of the dissolved carbon dioxide in a bottle of sparkling wine is about 10 atmospheres of pressure.

12. _____ In many bottles of sparkling wine, the cork is held in place by a wire cage known as a *muselet*.

13. _____ The tank process of sparkling wine production is used to create a wine that emphasizes youthful, floral, and primary fruit aromas.

14. _____ The most expensive method of making a sparkling wine is to inject carbon dioxide directly into a still wine.

15. _____ Chenin Blanc is often used to create sparkling wines in the Loire Valley.

1. Which of the following styles of sparkling wine has the highest level of potential residual sugar?
   a. Brut
   b. Demi-sec
   c. Extra dry
   d. Sec

2. Which of the following bottles is the largest?
   a. Magnum
   b. Rehoboam
   c. Jeroboam
   d. Nebuchadnezzar

3. Which of the following is added to a bottle of sparkling wine after the wine is disgorged?
   a. Liqueur d'expédition
   b. Cuve close
   c. Transversage
   d. Liqueur de tirage

4. Which of the following styles of sparkling wine is made using just white grape varieties?
   a. Cava
   b. Blanc de Noirs
   c. Blanc de Blancs
   d. Nonvintage

5. Which of the following styles of Champagne is most likely to be considered a brand's "house style" and most consistent wine?
   a. Vintage
   b. Blanc de Blancs
   c. Rosé
   d. Nonvintage

6. Which of the following terms is used to describe the second fermentation of a bottle of Traditional Method sparkling wine?
   a. Débourbage
   b. Prise de mousse
   c. Transversage
   d. Assemblage

7. What is a pupitre?
   a. A wooden rack used to hold bottles of sparkling wine during the riddling process
   b. A large machine used to mechanically rotate bottles of sparkling wine before disgorging
   c. A table used for sorting grapes prior to the crush
   d. A term used to describe the last juice pressed from grapes; destined to be used in the production of sweet sparkling wines.

8. Which of the following is the most accurate definition of a tête de cuvee wine?
   a. A sparkling wine that undergoes a second fermentation in the bottle
   b. The top-of-the-line sparkling wine produced by a given brand or producer
   c. A vintage sparkling wine made from 100% Chardonnay grapes
   d. A sparkling wine produced via assemblage

9. What is the French term for riddling?
   a. Autolysis
   b. Assemblage
   c. Remuage
   d. Cuve close

10. Which of the following represents the steps in the Traditional Method of sparkling wine production in the proper order?
    a. First fermentation, blending, bottling, second fermentation, riddling, disgorging, dosage
    b. First fermentation, bottling, second fermentation, blending, riddling, disgorging, dosage
    c. First fermentation, blending, second fermentation, bottling, dosage, riddling, disgorging
    d. First fermentation, bottling, second fermentation, dosage, riddling, blending, disgorging

FORTIFIED WINE PRODUCTION

LEARNING OBJECTIVES

After studying this chapter, the candidate should be able to:

- Recall the historical purpose for fortifying wines.
- Discuss how the fortified winemaking process differs from standard table wine production.

- Recognize the differences in the production methods of sweet and dry fortified wines.
- Identify the grape varieties commonly used in fortified wines.
- Describe how the solera system works.

43

EXERCISE 1: FORTIFIED WINE PRODUCTION: MATCHING

Fill in the blanks by matching each of the following fortified wines with its country or region of origin. Terms may be used more than once.

France   Spain   Cyprus   Greece   Italy   Portugal   Australia

1. _____   Commandaria

2. _____   Marsala

3. _____   Mavrodaphne of Patras

4. _____   Banyuls

5. _____   Rutherglen Muscat

6. _____   Muscat de Beaumes-de-Venise

7. _____   Port

8. _____   Madeira

9. _____   Málaga

10. _____   Setúbal

11. _____   Rasteau

12. _____   Maury

Fill in the blanks or give a short answer for the following statements or questions.

1. What is the term used for the process of fortified wine production in which alcohol is added to a fermenting wine while it still has a significant amount of sugar in it?

   _____

2. What grape variety is most widely used in the production of Sherry?

   _____

3. What two grape varieties are most commonly used in the production of dry styles of Madeira?

   _____

4. What style of Sherry is aged in the presence of flor yeast?

   _____

5. What style of Sherry is aged without the presence of flor yeast?

   _____

6. What type of aging occurs as a result of flor yeast?

   _____

7. What type of aging occurs when Sherry is allowed direct exposure to air?

   _____

8. What is the name of the complex network of barrels that is used to age Sherry?

   _____

9. What specific term is used for a French wine made by fortifying unfermented grape juice or must?

   _____

10. Where is Banyuls produced?

   _____

1. Which of the following is a fortified wine produced in Italy?
   a. Marsala
   b. Pineau des Charentes
   c. Setúbal
   d. Málaga

2. Sherry is aged and blended using a complex network of barrels known collectively as:
   a. Lagares
   b. The criadera system
   c. The chai
   d. The solera system

3. What style of Sherry is aged in the presence of flor yeast?
   a. Muscat Sherry
   b. Fino Sherry
   c. Cream Sherry
   d. Oloroso Sherry

4. Which of the following is a vin doux naturel produced in France?
   a. Setúbal
   b. Muscat de Beaumes-de-Venise
   c. Coteaux du Layon
   d. Sauternes

5. Which of the following fortified wines is a specialty of Cyprus?
   a. Rutherglen Muscat
   b. Rasteau
   c. Commandaria
   d. Maury

6. Which of the following is produced in the Cognac region?
   a. Muscat de Beaumes-de-Venise
   b. Commandaria
   c. Málaga
   d. Pineau des Charentes

7. The process of adding alcohol to a batch of fermenting wine while it still contains a significant amount of sugar is known by which of the following terms?
   a. Assemblage
   b. Mutage
   c. Oxidation
   d. Maceration

8. Which of the following is true concerning oloroso Sherry?
   a. It is made using a blend of red and white grapes.
   b. It is allowed to undergo oxidative aging.
   c. It is generally light in body and pale in color as compared to other styles of Sherry.
   d. It is aged in the presence of flor yeast.

9. Which of the following grape varieties is most widely used in the production of dry Madeira?
   a. Pedro Ximénez
   b. Palomino
   c. Airén
   d. Sercial

10. Which of the following grape varieties is most widely used in the production of Sherry?
    a. Palomino
    b. Tempranillo
    c. Pedro Ximénez
    d. Garnacha

WINE LABELS, LAWS, AND REGIONS

UNIT THREE

INTRODUCTION TO THE WORLD WINE INDUSTRY

CHAPTER EIGHT

LEARNING OBJECTIVES

After studying this chapter, the candidate should be able to:

- Understand how the history of wine relates to the current state of the wine industry.
- Describe the differences between the Old World and the New World of wine.

- Recall the different categories of wine.
- Recognize how geography and climate affect wine production in the various countries of Europe.
- Discuss the European Union system for designating wine quality and the EU labeling laws.

EXERCISE 1: LEGALLY DEFINED WINE REGIONS: MATCHING

Fill in the blanks by matching each of the following legally defined wine regions with its country of origin. Terms may be used more than once.

Spain   Portugal   Italy   Australia   France   Germany   South Africa   United States

1. _____ Geographical Indication

2. _____ Denominación de Origen

3. _____ Wine of Origin

4. _____ Prädikatswein

5. _____ Denominazione di Origine Controllata

6. _____ Appellation d'Origine Contrôlée

7. _____ Indicazione Geographica Tipica

8. _____ Vino de Pago

9. _____ AVA

10. _____ Vinho Regional

Fill in the blanks or give a short answer for the following statements or questions.

1. The European Union was founded in _____ as an economic initiative to help relatively

   small countries compete with larger economies in the _____.

2. Approximately _____% of the global vineyard is located in Europe.

3. According to the International Organization of Vine and Wine (OIV), what were the top three wine-producing countries in 2018?

   _____

   _____.

4. Under the new EU framework, the highest level of wine classification available is PDO, which stands for

   _____

   _____.

5. The new EU regulations permit the continuing use of pre-existing designations of origin, as long as they were registered prior to

   _____.

6. The second tier of quality wine under the new EU classification system is known as PGI, which stands for

   _____

   _____.

7. If a protected place-name is used on the label of a PDO wine, _____% of the grapes in the wine must be from the stated region.

8. If a protected place-name is used on the label of a PGI wine, _____% of the grapes in the wine must be from the stated region.

9. If a PDO or PGI wine states a vintage date on the label, _____% of the wine must be from the stated vintage.

10. If a PDO or PGI wine uses the name of a single grape variety as its name, _____% of the wine must be from made from the stated variety.

For each of the following wine regions, production techniques, or wine styles, determine whether they are most representative of the New World or Old World style of wine. Place a check mark in the column of the style that is *most* representative of the term.

Wine Region, Production Technique, or Wine Style:	Old World?	New World?
1. Bold flavors	☐	☐
2. Emphasis on terroir	☐	☐
3. Vineyards planted close to markets	☐	☐
4. Highlight the style or skill of the winemaker	☐	☐
5. More subtlety	☐	☐
6. Emphasis on fruit flavors	☐	☐
7. Less acidity	☐	☐
8. Wines of California	☐	☐
9. Lower levels of alcohol	☐	☐
10. Subtle flavors	☐	☐
11. Emphasis on grape variety	☐	☐
12. Wines of Italy	☐	☐
13. More alcohol	☐	☐
14. Higher acidity	☐	☐
15. Earthier flavors	☐	☐

1. Which year best represents the beginning of the phylloxera crisis in Europe?
   a. 1650
   b. 1720
   c. 1860
   d. 1970

2. Which of the following is a typical attribute of an Old World style of wine?
   a. Fruit-forward flavors
   b. Emphasis on grape variety
   c. Higher levels of alcohol
   d. Emphasis on terroir

3. Which of the following is a typical attribute of a New World style of wine?
   a. Higher acidity
   b. Higher levels of alcohol
   c. Earthier flavors
   d. Subtlety

4. Under the new EU wine categorization scheme, traditional wine classifications such as France's AOC and Italy's DOCG may continue to be used, as long as the categories were registered by which of the following dates?
   a. December 31, 2009
   b. December 31, 2011
   c. January 1, 2013
   d. January 1, 2014

5. What country uses the Wine of Origin scheme to categorize its quality wines?
   a. Australia
   b. Argentina
   c. The United States
   d. South Africa

6. In the EU, if a protected place-name is used on the label of a PDO wine, what minimum percentage of the wine must be from the stated region?
   a. 100%
   b. 95%
   c. 85%
   d. 75%

7. When did the wine competition now known as the "Judgment of Paris" take place?
   a. 1875
   b. 1926
   c. 1976
   d. 1651

8. If a wine is labeled as "Pinot Grigio della Venezie IGT," what minimum percentage of the wine must be made using Pinot Grigio grapes?
   a. 100%
   b. 95%
   c. 85%
   d. 75%

9. Brokers, importers, and exporters of wine are considered to represent which of the following portions of the wine industry?
   a. Distributors
   b. Producers
   c. Retailers
   d. Regulators

10. Which of the following represents the quality tiers used for EU wines, starting with the lowest quality tier and moving up?
    a. PDO, PGI, Wine
    b. Wine, PDO, PGI
    c. PGI, Wine, PDO
    d. Wine, PGI, PDO

FRANCE

CHAPTER NINE

LEARNING OBJECTIVES

After studying this chapter, the candidate should be able to:

- Identify the general role and position of France in the global wine industry.
- Recall the geographical location and general climate of France's major wine regions.

- Discuss the hierarchy of wine designations used in France.
- Recall which grape varieties and wine styles are associated with France's important appellations.
- Describe the classification systems of the major wine regions of France.

EXERCISE 1: INTRODUCTION TO FRENCH WINES: SHORT ANSWER/FILL IN THE BLANK

Fill in the blanks or give a short answer for the following statements or questions.

1. What French wine region was greatly impacted by the 12th century marriage of Eleanor of Aquitaine to Henry II?

   _____

2. Which French wine region, situated on the border with Germany, has a history of alternating between French and German control?

   _____

3. What term is used to refer to the elevated region located in the central portion of France?

   _____

   _____

4. What is the most widely planted white wine grape variety in France?

   _____

5. What is the most widely planted red wine grape variety in France?

   _____

6. What term is used for a basic French table wine made using 100% French grapes?

   _____

7. How many regional Vin de Pays categories are there currently in France?

   _____

   _____

Using the map below, identify the wine regions of France.

Cahors
Burgundy
Jurançon
Alsace
Savoie

Provence
Bordeaux
Gaillac
Béarn
Chablis

Loire Valley
Champagne
Rhône Valley
Jura
Madiran

Languedoc
Corsica
Beaujolais
Roussillon

Figure 9-1: Map Exercise – Wine Regions of France

1. _____

2. _____

3. _____

4. _____

5. _____

6. _____

7. _____

8. _____

9. _____

10. _____

11. _____

12. _____

13. _____

14. _____

15. _____

16. _____

17. _____

18. _____

19. _____

Match each of the following terms with its appropriate definition. Each term will be used only once.

Merlot   Malbec   Garonne   Château Haut-Brion
Cabernet Sauvignon   En primeur   Dordogne   Château Mouton-Rothschild
Sauvignon Blanc   Muscadelle   Gironde   Château d'Yquem
Sémillon   Cabernet Franc   Château Cheval Blanc

1. _____ The most widely planted red grape variety in the area of Entre-Deux-Mers

2. _____ A St.-Émilion Grand Cru Classé–Category "A" property

3. _____ The grape variety that forms the basis for most dry white Bordeaux wines

4. _____ A property whose ranking on the Bordeaux Classification of 1855 was changed in 1973

5. _____ Term that represents the Bordeaux tradition of selling wine in futures

6. _____ A superior first growth for sweet Bordeaux

7. _____ The grape variety that generally forms the basis for sweet Bordeaux wines such as Sauternes

8. _____ The river that flows past the city of Bordeaux and forms the border between Graves and Entre-Deux-Mers

9. _____ A minor white grape variety of Bordeaux

10. _____ The third most widely planted red grape variety in Bordeaux

11. _____ The river that flows past the city of Libourne

12. _____ The leading red grape variety of the Left Bank

13. _____ The only château from Graves that was rated premier cru in the 1855 Classification of red wines

14. _____ A minor red grape of Bordeaux

15. _____ An estuary that flows through the region of Bordeaux out to the Atlantic

Using the map and the terms listed below, identify the wine regions of Bordeaux.

Barsac
Margaux
Cérons
Fronsac
Graves
Saint-Émilion

Entre-Deux-Mers
Loupiac
Pessac-Léognan
Côtes de Bourg
Haut-Médoc
Pomerol

Graves de Vayres
Sainte Foy-Côtes de
  Bordeaux
Sauternes
Haut-Benauge
Listrac-Médoc

Moulis-en-Médoc
Saint-Estèphe
Pauillac
Saint-Julien

Map Exercise: Bordeaux

Copyright: The Society of Wine Educators

Figure 9-2: Map Exercise – Bordeaux

1. _____
2. _____
3. _____
4. _____
5. _____
6. _____
7. _____
8. _____
9. _____
10. _____
11. _____
12. _____
13. _____
14. _____
15. _____
16. _____
17. _____
18. _____
19. _____
20. _____
21. _____

EXERCISE 5: LEFT BANK, RIGHT BANK, OR ENTRE-DEUX-MERS?

For each of the following areas, determine whether they are located in the Left Bank, Right Bank, or Entre-Deux-Mers. Place a check mark in the correct column.

Region	Left Bank?	Right Bank?	Entre-Deux-Mers?
1. The city of Bordeaux	☐	☐	☐
2. Graves	☐	☐	☐
3. St.-Julien	☐	☐	☐
4. Fronsac	☐	☐	☐
5. Graves de Vayres	☐	☐	☐
6. Pauillac	☐	☐	☐
7. St.-Estèphe	☐	☐	☐
8. St.-Émilion	☐	☐	☐
9. Pessac-Léognan	☐	☐	☐
10. The Libournais	☐	☐	☐
11. The Médoc	☐	☐	☐
12. Pomerol	☐	☐	☐
13. Castillon-Côtes de Bordeaux	☐	☐	☐
14. Loupiac	☐	☐	☐

Using the map below, identify the following subregions and appellations of the Loire.

Touraine   Chinon   Pays Nantais   Bourgueil
Pouilly-Fumé   Anjou-Saumur   Upper Loire
Savennières   Vouvray   Sancerre

1. _____

2. _____

3. _____

4. _____

5. _____

6. _____

7. _____

8. _____

9. _____

10. _____

Map Exercise: Loire Valley

Copyright: The Society of Wine Educators 2016

Figure 9-3: Map Exercise – Loire Valley

EXERCISE 7: THE LOIRE VALLEY: KEY WHITE GRAPES

Place each of the following wine regions in the appropriate column based on the main white grape variety used in each area.

Reuilly   Bonnezeaux   Montlouis-sur-Loire   Muscadet
Pays Nantais   Menetou-Salon   Sancerre   Quarts-de-Chaume
Savennières   Vouvray   Pouilly-Fumé   Quincy

Sauvignon Blanc	Chenin Blanc	Melon de Bourgogne

Fill in the blanks or give a short answer for the following statements or questions.

1. What name is often used in the Pays Nantais for the Pinot Gris grape variety?

   _____

2. What winemaking procedure is often used in the Pays Nantais to make the Melon de Bourgogne-based wines taste richer and more complex?

   _____

3. What is the main grape variety used in the red wines of Chinon? _____

4. What is the main grape variety used in the red wines of Sancerre?_____

5. What marketing term is often used for the sparkling wines of the Loire?_____

   _____

6. Name three Anjou wine appellations that are known for sweet white wines:

   _____

   _____

7. What wine is the first (and only) grand cru of the Loire? _____

   _____

8. Put the following wines in order of typical sweetness, from driest to sweetest: Rosé d'Anjou, Cabernet d'Anjou, Rosé de Loire.

   _____

9. What Loire Valley white wine is often called "the most cerebral wine in the world"?

   _____

10. What is another name for Pineau de la Loire? _____

11. What grape variety goes by the name Côt? _____

12. What grape variety goes by the name Breton?_____

13. What are the three leading red wine appellations of Touraine?

   _____

Fill in the blanks or give a short answer for the following statements or questions.

1. Name the five main zones that make up the Champagne appellation: _____

_____

_____

2. What is the name of the chalky soil that underlies much of the Côte des Bar? _____

_____

3. Name the three main grape varieties grown in the Champagne region: _____

_____

4. Name the four minor grape varieties grown in the Champagne region: _____

_____

5. What term is used to describe the juice used in the highest-quality sparkling wines?

_____

6. What term is used to describe the juice (often used in demi-sec and extra-dry sparkling wines) from the second set of pressings?

_____

7. What terms are used to describe the remaining juice that may be used to produce still wines or other products?

_____

8. What is the French term for vintage Champagne? _____

_____

9. What term may be found on the label of a grower Champagne? _____

_____

10. What types of wine are produced in the Coteaux Champenois AOC?_____

_____

11. What AOC covers rosé wines produced in the far south end of the Champagne region? _____

_____

Mark each of the following statements as true or false.

1. _____ Alsace is located across the Rhine River from the German wine region of Baden and south of the Pfalz.

2. _____ Alsace is primarily white grape territory, with Pinot Noir and Cabernet Franc being the only red grape varieties permitted in the AOC wines of the region.

3. _____ There are four types of appellations in Alsace: Alsace AOC, Alsace Premier Cru AOC, Alsace Grand Cru AOC, and Crémant d'Alsace.

4. _____ The Klevener grape variety is allowed for use in Alsace AOC wines, but it may only be grown in selected areas.

5. _____ Chasselas, Auxerrois, and Pinot Gris are all permitted grape varieties for use in Alsace AOC wines.

6. _____ There are presently 65 grand cru vineyards in Alsace.

7. _____ Gewurztraminer, Muscat, Pinot Gris, and Riesling are considered to be the four "noble grapes" of Alsace.

8. _____ The majority of the Alsace Grand Cru vineyards are located in the Bas-Rhin area.

9. _____ Due to the rain shadow of the Vosges Mountains, Alsace is one of the driest parts of France.

10. _____ Pinot Noir, Pinot Gris, and Pinot Blanc are all allowed to be grown in the Alsace AOC.

11. _____ Crémant d'Alsace accounts for approximately 45% of all wine produced in Alsace.

12. _____ Blended wines are not common in Alsace, but they are permitted to be labeled using the term *Edelzwicker*.

13. _____ The term *Gentil* may be used on the label of a blended wine from Alsace provided the wine contains a minimum of 50% noble grape varieties.

14. _____ A wine from Alsace labeled with the term *Vendage Tardive* must be produced as an ultra-sweet wine.

15. _____ A Pinot d'Alsace wine may be produced using Pinot Noir grapes, but it must be vinified as a white wine.

Using the map and the terms listed below, identify the following wine areas and towns of Burgundy.

Côte de Beaune	Hautes-Côtes de Beaune	Nuits-Saint-Georges	Hautes-Côtes de Nuits
Tournus	Mâconnais	Côte Chalonnaise	Chablis
Côte de Nuits	Dijon	Beaune	Mâcon

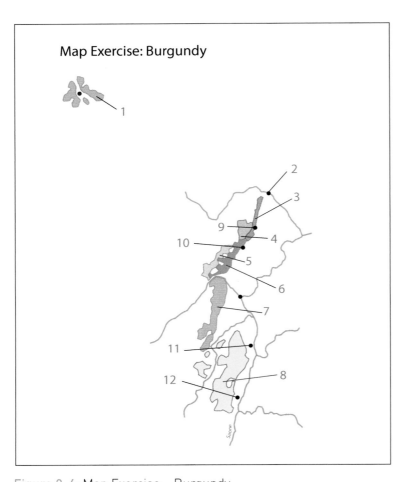

Map Exercise: Burgundy

1. _____

2. _____

3. _____

4. _____

5. _____

6. _____

7. _____

8. _____

9. _____

10. _____

11. _____

12. _____

Figure 9-4: Map Exercise – Burgundy

Match the following numbers with the descriptive statements below. Each number may be used more than once.

7	17	33	90	254
8	24	60	103	
14	32	80	129	

	Number	Definition
1.		Number of acres in the Chablis Grand Cru vineyard
2.		Percentage of Côte de Nuits production that is Pinot Noir
3.		Approximate number of miles from Chablis to the Côte d'Or
4.		Number of grand cru vineyards in the Côte de Nuits
5.		Percentage of Burgundy's annual output that is Chardonnay
6.		Number of sub-appellations in the (regional) Bourgogne AOC
7.		Number of grand cru vineyards in the Côte d'Or
8.		Total number of Burgundy grand cru vineyards
9.		Number of principal premier cru vineyards in Chablis
10.		Number of grand cru vineyards in the Côte de Beaune
11.		Number of hectares in the Chablis Grand Cru vineyard
12.		Approximate number of kilometers from Chablis to the Côte d'Or
13.		Number of grand cru vineyards in the Côte de Beaune that produce white wine only

Using the map and the terms listed below, identify the following communes of the Côte de Nuits.

Vougeot
Chambolle-Musigny
Nuits-Saint-Georges

Brochon
Morey-Saint-Denis
Marsannay

Flagey-Échezeaux
Vosne-Romanée
Corgoloin

Fixin
Gevry-Chambertin
Comblanchien

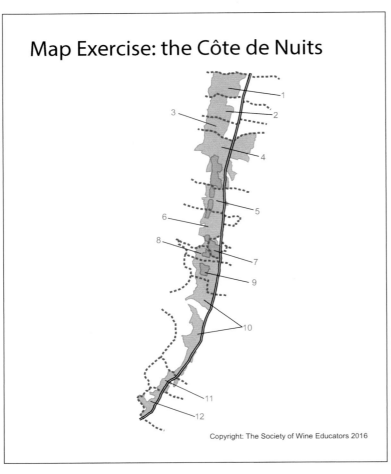

Map Exercise: the Côte de Nuits

Copyright: The Society of Wine Educators 2016

1. _____

2. _____

3. _____

4. _____

5. _____

6. _____

7. _____

8. _____

9. _____

10. _____

11. _____

12. _____

Figure 9-5: Map Exercise – Côte de Nuits

Match each of the following terms with its appropriate definition. Each term will be used only once.

Corton Clos de Vougeot Climat Mercurey
Côte de Nuits Aligoté Grand cru La Tâche
Montrachet Marsannay Côte de Beaune Pinot Noir
Chardonnay Gamay Premier cru

1. _____ Minor red grape variety of Burgundy; grown primarily in the Mâconnais

2. _____ Area located in the northern end of the Côte d'Or

3. _____ Term used in Burgundy to refer to officially designated small plots of land

4. _____ The largest communal AOC located in the Côte Chalonnaise

5. _____ Commune appellation located in the Côte de Nuits

6. _____ White grape variety used in the wines of the Bouzeron AOC

7. _____ Area located on the southern end of the Côte d'Or

8. _____ Grape variety used in Pouilly-Fuissé and St.-Véran

9. _____ Highest ranking awarded to designated vineyards in Burgundy

10. _____ Grand cru vineyard with over 80 individual owners

11. _____ The only grand cru vineyard located in the Côte de Beaune that produces both red and white wine

12. _____ The main grape variety of the Côte de Nuits

13. _____ Second highest ranking awarded to designated vineyards in Burgundy

14. _____ Grand cru vineyard in the Côte de Beaune that produces white wine only

15. _____ Grand cru vineyard located in the commune of Vosne-Romanée

Using the map and the terms listed below, identify the following wine areas of the Côte de Beaune.

Saint-Romain   Chorey-lès-Beaune   Pernand-Vergelesses   Aloxe-Corton
Meursault   Volnay   Beaune   Savigny-lès-Beaune
Pommard   Puligny-Montrachet   Chassagne-Montrachet   Monthélie
Saint-Aubin   Auxey-Duresses   Santenay

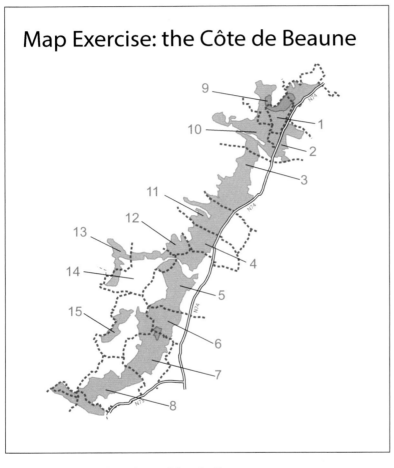

Figure 9-6: Map Exercise – Côte de Beaune

1. _____

2. _____

3. _____

4. _____

5. _____

6. _____

7. _____

8. _____

9. _____

10. _____

11. _____

12. _____

13. _____

14. _____

15. _____

EXERCISE 16: BURGUNDY: TRUE OR FALSE

Mark each of the following statements as true or false.

1. _____ Two grand cru vineyards are located in the Côte Chalonnaise.

2. _____ Due to the influence of the French Revolution and the Napoleonic Code, many vineyards in Burgundy have multiple owners.

3. _____ The Mâconnais lies directly north of Beaujolais.

4. _____ Only 10% of the total production of the Côte de Beaune is red wine.

5. _____ The name of the commune is generally listed first on the label of a Burgundy Premier Cru.

6. _____ The Mâcon-Villages AOC appellation is only designated for white wine.

7. _____ Burgundy is larger in area and produces more wine than Bordeaux.

8. _____ The weather in Chablis, with cold winters and cool summers, often makes it difficult to fully ripen grapes.

9. _____ Burgundy grands crus often use the term "1er Cru" on the label.

10. _____ Santenay is the largest communal AOC in the Côte Chalonnaise.

11. _____ Négociant trade represents about three-quarters of Burgundy's annual wine output.

12. _____ Chardonnay is the only grape variety permitted to be used in Chablis.

13. _____ All of the grand cru vineyards in the Côte de Nuits make red wine exclusively, with the exception of Musigny, which also produces a small amount of white.

14. _____ Fourchaume is a well-known Chablis Premier Cru vineyard.

15. _____ While primarily known for dry, still wines, Burgundy also produces a small amount of sparkling wine.

16. _____ Sauvignon Blanc is not approved for use in any of the AOC wines of Burgundy.

The following chart lists some of the most famous of the Burgundy Grand Cru vineyards. For each vineyard, state the commune(s) in which it is located, and whether it produces red or white wines (or both). The first row has been filled in as an example.

	Grand Cru Vineyard	Commune(s)	Red, White, or Both?
1.	Montrachet	Puligny-Montrachet and Chassagne-Montrachet	White
2.	La Grande Rue		
3.	Bonnes Mares		
4.	Romanée-Conti		
5.	Clos de la Roche		
6.	Corton		
7.	Musigny		
8.	Richebourg		
9.	Échezeaux		
10.	Corton-Charlemagne		
11.	Clos de Vougeot		
12.	La Tâche		
13.	Chambertin		

Using the map and the terms listed below, identify the wine areas of Beaujolais.

Régnié

Chénas

Brouilly

Morgon

Côte de Brouilly

Juliénas

Moulin-à-Vent

Chiroubles

Beaujolais-Villages

Beaujolais AOC

Saint-Amour

Fleurie

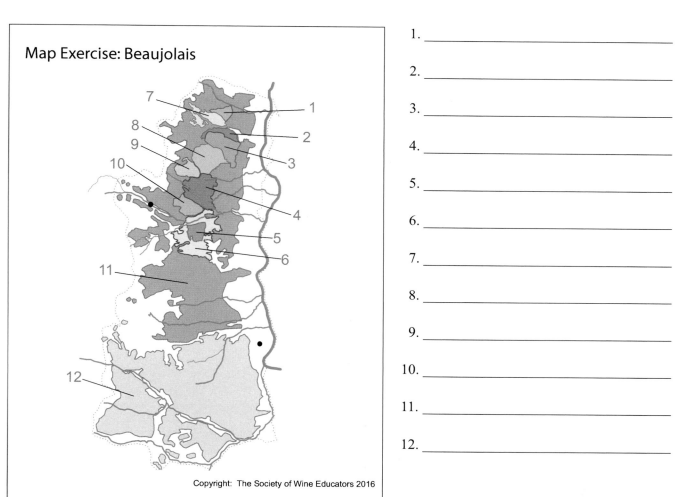

Map Exercise: Beaujolais

Copyright: The Society of Wine Educators 2016

1. _____

2. _____

3. _____

4. _____

5. _____

6. _____

7. _____

8. _____

9. _____

10. _____

11. _____

12. _____

Figure 9-7: Map Exercise – Beaujolais

Fill in the blanks or give a short answer for the following statements or questions.

1. The northern portion of the Beaujolais AOC is known for its _____ soils, which have proven ideal for the _____ grape variety.

2. The Beaujolais AOC is located to the west of the _____ River.

3. Some styles of Beaujolais have bright red and tropical fruit flavors, which may be the result of the _____ fermentation process that is often used in the region.

4. Beaujolais Nouveau is released every year on the third _____ of _____.

5. The boundaries of the Beaujolais region actually overlap slightly with those of the _____ region.

6. While the majority of the grapes grown in Beaujolais are Gamay, other grapes planted in the region include:
    _____
    _____.

7. There are a total of _____ villages in Beaujolais that are allowed to produce wines labeled with the term "Beaujolais-Villages AOC."

8. Name the three Beaujolais crus that are known for producing lighter styles of the wine:
    _____
    _____

9. Name the four Beaujolais crus that are known for producing medium- to fuller-bodied styles of the wine:
    _____
    _____

10. Name the three Beaujolais crus that are known for creating age-worthy styles of the wine:
    _____
    _____

Using the map and the terms listed below, identify the wine areas of the Rhône Valley.

Vacqueyras

Ventoux

Hermitage

Château-Grillet

Lirac

Côte-Rôtie

Grignan-les-Adhémar

Rasteau

Cornas

Gigondas

Luberon

Saint-Péray

Châteauneuf-du-Pape

Vinsobres

Crozes-Hermitage

Beaumes-de-Venise

Condrieu

Saint-Joseph

Tavel

Cairanne

Figure 9-8: Map Exercise – The Rhône Valley

1. _____

2. _____

3. _____

4. _____

5. _____

6. _____

7. _____

8. _____

9. _____

10. _____

11. _____

12. _____

13. _____

14. _____

15. _____

16. _____

17. _____

18. _____

19. _____

20. _____

Match each of the following terms with its appropriate definition. Each term will be used only once.

Côte Rotie	Syrah	St.-Joseph	Marsanne
Tavel	Grenache	Rasteau	Clairette
Galet	Cornas	Viognier	
Mistral	Château Grillet	Grenache Blanc	

1. _____ The dominant white grape variety of the southern Rhône

2. _____ Small AOC located within the larger Condrieu AOC

3. _____ Region known for producing red vin doux naturel based on Grenache

4. _____ A rounded stone that covers the ground in some parts of the Rhône Valley

5. _____ White grape variety used to make sparkling wines with the Méthode Ancestrale Dioise

6. _____ An AOC in the northern Rhône that requires wines to be 100% Syrah

7. _____ The strong, cold wind of the Rhône and surrounding regions

8. _____ One of the larger red wine AOCs of the Northern Rhône Valley

9. _____ A white grape variety that is used, in small amounts, in the red wines of Hermitage and some of the surrounding areas

10. _____ An AOC in the southern Rhône that produces rosé exclusively

11. _____ The main red grape variety of the northern Rhône

12. _____ The northernmost appellation in the Northern Rhône Valley

13. _____ The grape variety used in Condrieu

14. _____ The main red grape variety of the southern Rhône

Using the map and the terms listed below, identify the wine areas of the Languedoc-Roussillon region.

Muscat de Saint-Jean-de-Minervois
Malepère
Minervois
Quatourze
Faugères
Muscat de Mireval
Saint-Chinian
Limoux

Cabrières
Maury
Fitou
Muscat de Frontignan
La Clape
Rivesaltes
Banyuls
St.-Georges d'Orques

Clairette du Languedoc
Cabardès
Pic Saint-Loup
Gres de Montpellier
Picpoul de Pinet
Terrasses du Larzac
Corbières

Figure 9-9: Map Exercise – The Languedoc-Roussillon

1. _____

2. _____

3. _____

4. _____

5. _____

6. _____

7. _____

8. _____

9. _____

10. _____

11. _____

12. _____

13. _____

14. _____

15. _____

16. _____

17. _____

18. _____

19. _____

20. _____

21. _____

22. _____

23. _____

Match each of the following terms with its appropriate definition. Each term will be used only once.

Bandol   Cahors   Madiran   Corbières
Minervois   Terrasses du Larzac   Limoux   Nielluccio
Côtes de Provence   Rivesaltes   Arrufiac   Vermentino
Fer Servadou   Sainte-Victoire

1. _____   AOC in Southwest France that produces red wines based on the Malbec grape variety

2. _____   Large AOC within Provence, well-known for rosé production

3. _____   White grape variety grown in Southwest France

4. _____   AOC in Provence known for deep reds and hearty rosés based on the Mourvèdre grape variety

5. _____   Area in the Languedoc-Roussillon known for sparkling wines

6. _____   Red grape variety grown in Southwest France

7. _____   AOC in the Languedoc approved in July of 2014

8. _____   The largest AOC of the Languedoc-Roussillon in terms of production

9. _____   AOC in Southwest France that produces red wines based on the Tannat grape variety

10. _____   AOC located just to the north of the Corbières AOC

11. _____   Sub-appellation of the Côtes de Provence AOC

12. _____   Area in the Roussillon known for fortified wines made with the Muscat grape variety

13. _____   White grape variety used in the Vin de Corse AOC

14. _____   Red grape variety (otherwise known as *Sangiovese*) used in the Vin de Corse AOC

1. Which of the following wines is produced using Sauvignon Blanc?
   a. Muscadet
   b. Vouvray
   c. Fleurie
   d. Sancerre

2. Which of the following regions, known for white wines, is located in the northern section of Graves?
   a. Fronsac
   b. Bourgueil
   c. Pessac-Léognan
   d. Vallée de la Marne

3. Which of the following grape varieties are all part of the red Bordeaux blend?
   a. Cabernet Sauvignon, Cabernet Franc, Malbec, Merlot, and Petit Verdot
   b. Cabernet Sauvignon, Cabernet Franc, Malbec, Merlot, and Pinot Noir
   c. Cabernet Sauvignon, Ruby Franc, Malbec, Merlot, and Petit Verdot
   d. Cabernet Sauvignon, Cabernet Franc, Malbec, Syrah, and Petit Verdot

4. Which of the following is the highest-quality appellation of Chablis?
   a. Chablis Premier Cru
   b. Chablis Grand Cru
   c. Chablis Cru Classé
   d. Chablis Premier Grand Cru

5. Which of the following areas is located just *south* of the Côte de Beaune?
   a. The Côte de Nuits
   b. The Côte Chalonnaise
   c. The Mâconnais
   d. Beaujolais

6. Which of the following regions produces Muscadet?
   a. Anjou-Saumur
   b. Touraine
   c. The Upper Loire
   d. The Pays Nantais

7. What is the dominant red grape variety of the southern Rhône Valley?
   a. Grenache
   b. Syrah
   c. Carignan
   d. Viognier

8. Which of the following communes is located farthest *north*?
   a. Gevry-Chambertin
   b. Vougeot
   c. Fixin
   d. Vosne-Romanée

9. Which of the following grape varieties is used in the production of Morgon?
   a. Pinot Noir
   b. Chardonnay
   c. Syrah
   d. Gamay

10. Which of the following is a small AOC located within the larger Condrieu AOC?
    a. Cornas
    b. Château-Grillet
    c. Lirac
    d. Rasteau

11. Which of the following AOCs produces 100% rosé wine?
    a. Tavel
    b. St.-Péray
    c. Clairette de Die
    d. Brouilly

12. Which of the following wines is made with a majority of Mourvèdre?
    a. Cahors
    b. Madiran
    c. Nuits-Saint-Georges
    d. Bandol

13. What percentage of the output of the wines of Provence is rosé?
    a. 25%
    b. 56%
    c. 88%
    d. 95%

14. Which of the following is a Beaujolais cru?
    a. Sancerre
    b. Brouilly
    c. Touraine
    d. Bourguiel

15. What type of wine is produced at Château d'Yquem?
    a. Right Bank Bordeaux
    b. Red Burgundy
    c. Sauternes
    d. Champagne

16. What term may be found on the label of a grower Champagne?
    a. Négociant manipulant
    b. Marche d'acheteur
    c. Récoltant manipulant
    d. Marque auxiliaire

17. Which of the following appellations is located on the Right Bank of Bordeaux?
    a. Fronsac
    b. Cérons
    c. Pauillac
    d. Margaux

18. Which of the following was the only château from Graves that was rated premier cru in the 1855 Classification of Bordeaux?
    a. Château Margaux
    b. Château Latour
    c. Château Montrose
    d. Château Haut-Brion

19. Which of the following grape varieties is used in the production of Montrachet?
    a. Sauvignon Blanc
    b. Chardonnay
    c. Pinot Noir
    d. Malbec

20. What are the three main grape varieties grown in Champagne?
    a. Pinot Noir, Meunier, and Chardonnay
    b. Chardonnay, Pinot Gris, and Pinot Noir
    c. Meunier, Pinot Blanc, and Chenin Blanc
    d. Chenin Blanc, Chardonnay, and Pinot Noir

21. What area is covered by the Méditerranée IGP?
    a. Bordeaux
    b. The Loire
    c. Provence
    d. Chablis

22. Where is the Quarts de Chaume AOC located?
    a. Pays Nantais
    b. Anjou-Saumur
    c. Fréjus
    d. Côtes du Roussillon

ITALY

LEARNING OBJECTIVES

After studying this chapter, the candidate should be able to:

- Identify the general role and position of Italy in the global wine industry.
- Recall the physical location and general climate of Italy's major wine regions.
- Discuss the hierarchy of wine designations from vino to DOCG.

- Recall the grape varieties, wine styles, and important appellations in the Veneto, Piedmont, and Tuscany.
- Identify the major wine regions and grapes of other regions in Italy.

EXERCISE 1: ITALY – GRAPES AND GEOGRAPHY: TRUE OR FALSE

Mark each of the following statements as true or false.

1. _____ There is a considerable overall difference in climate between the cooler, northern portion of Italy and the hot, southern region.

2. _____ Very few parts of Italy are more than 75 miles from the sea.

3. _____ The Apennine Mountain Range forms most of the northern border of Italy.

4. _____ The rich valley of the Po River is a relatively flat area located in the southern section of Italy.

5. _____ The Alps form a solid wall that holds back most of the Arctic air masses that chill much of northern Europe in the winter.

6. _____ The Tyrrhenian Sea is located along the western coast of Italy.

7. _____ Tuscany is located along Italy's Adriatic Coast.

8. _____ The Ionian Sea is located on Italy's southern border, along the coastlines of Apulia, Basilicata, and Calabria.

9. _____ Sangiovese is the most widely planted red grape variety in Italy.

10. _____ Trebbiano, the most widely planted white wine grape variety in Italy, is the same grape known in France as Ugni Blanc.

Using the numbers 1–7 and the map and the terms listed below, identify the major cities of Italy.

Venice	Milan	Naples	Rome
Florence	Bologna	Turin	

Figure 10-1: Map Exercise – Italy

1. _____

2. _____

3. _____

4. _____

5. _____

6. _____

7. _____

Using the numbers 8–27 and the map and the terms listed below, identify the major wine-producing regions of Italy.

Emilia-Romagna	Liguria	Le Marche	Molise	Basilicata
Sicily	Calabria	Tuscany	Lombardy	Piedmont
Puglia	Trentino–Alto Adige	Umbria	Lazio	Abruzzo
Sardinia	Veneto	Campania	Valle d'Aosta	Friuli-Venezia Giulia

8. _____   15. _____   22. _____

9. _____   16. _____   23. _____

10. _____   17. _____   24. _____

11. _____   18. _____   25. _____

12. _____   19. _____   26. _____

13. _____   20. _____   27. _____

14. _____   21. _____

Fill in the missing information in the table below. The first row has been filled in as an example.

Appellation	Designation	Grape/Grapes	Style: Red, White, or Rosé; Dry or Sweet; Still or Sparkling
Amarone della Valpolicella	DOCG	Corvina, Corvinone, Rondinella	Red, dry, still
Recioto della Valpolicella			
Valpolicella			
Bardolino Superiore			
Bardolino Chiaretto			
Soave			
Recioto di Soave			
Asolo Prosecco			
Prosecco			

Using the map and the terms listed below, identify the major wine-producing areas of the Veneto.

Colli Berici DOC   Monti Lessini DOC   Breganze DOC   Bardolino DOC
Soave DOC   Lugana DOC   Lison-Pramaggiore DOC Bagnoli DOC
Valpolicella DOC   Asolo Prosecco DOCG   Gambellara DOC   Piave DOC
Colli Euganei DOC   Bianco di Custoza DOC   Vicenza DOC   Valdadige DOC
Coneglinao Valdobbiadene Prosecco DOCG

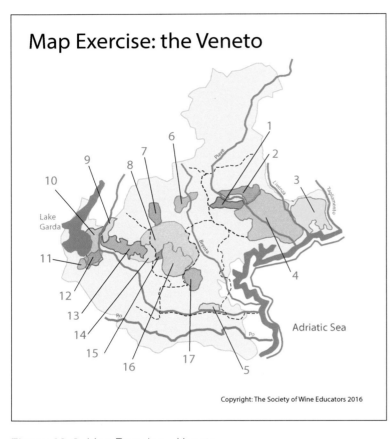

Figure 10-2: Map Exercise – Veneto

1. _____

2. _____

3. _____

4. _____

5. _____

6. _____

7. _____

8. _____

9. _____

10. _____

11. _____

12. _____

13. _____

14. _____

15. _____

16. _____

17. _____

Fill in the missing information in the table below. The first row has been filled in as an example.

Appellation	Designation	Grape/Grapes	Style: Red, White, or Rosé; Dry or Sweet; Still or Sparkling
Barolo	DOCG	Nebbiolo	Red, dry, still
Barbaresco			
Moscato d'Asti			
Asti			
Roero			
Gattinara			
Ghemme			
Gavi			
Barbera d'Alba			
Acqui			

Using the map and the terms listed below, identify the major wine-producing areas of Piedmont.

Freisa di Chieri DOC   Brachetto d'Acqui DOCG   Carema DOC   Lessona DOC
Gavi DOCG   Roero DOCG   Barolo DOCG   Ghemme DOCG
Nizza DOCG   Colli Tortonesi DOC   Boca DOC   Erbaluce di Caluso DOCG
Barbera d'Asti DOCG   Gattinara DOCG   Barbaresco DOCG

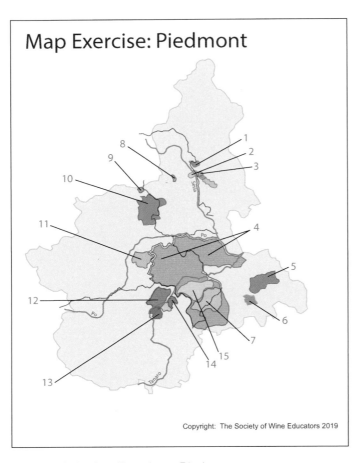

Copyright: The Society of Wine Educators 2019

Figure 10-3: Map Exercise – Piedmont

1. _____

2. _____

3. _____

4. _____

5. _____

6. _____

7. _____

8. _____

9. _____

10. _____

11. _____

12. _____

13. _____

14. _____

15. _____

Match each of the following terms with its appropriate definition. Each term will be used only once.

Appassimento	Sforzato	Valtellina	Inferno	Collio Goriziano
Südtirol	Chiavennasca	Ribolla Gialla	Spanna	Recioto
Satèn	Ripasso	Franciacorta	Metodo Classico	Langhe

1. _____ Grape variety often used in orange wines

2. _____ A winemaking process that uses partially dried grapes

3. _____ A blanc de blancs sparkling wine produced in Lombardy

4. _____ A local name for the Nebbiolo grape variety used in Lombardy

5. _____ One of the subzones of the Valtellina Superiore DOCG

6. _____ An alternative name often used for the Trentino-Alto Adige region

7. _____ A DOC, located in Friuli-Venezia Giulia, known for making white blends as well as orange wines

8. _____ A DOCG for sparkling wines from Lombardy

9. _____ Term often used in Italy to refer to the process used to create high-quality sparkling wines

10. _____ Term often used to refer to sweet wines made using grapes that are partially dried after harvest

11. _____ A local name for the Nebbiolo grape variety used in some parts of Piedmont

12. _____ A high-alcohol wine made using partially dried Nebbiolo grapes

13. _____ A region in Lombardy known for producing red wines using the Nebbiolo grape variety

14. _____ A traditional wine production technique that uses the sediment or lees from a previous batch in order to make a full-bodied wine

15. _____ A large DOC in Piedmont that covers many of the smaller regions, including Barolo, Barbaresco, and Roero

Fill in the blanks or give a short answer for the following statements or questions.

1. What are the three main cities of Tuscany? _____

   _____

2. Red wine makes up what percentage of the total output of Tuscan wine? _____

3. What term was created in response to the fact that 100% Sangiovese wines made in the Chianti region once had to be categorized as vino da tavola? _____

4. Basic Chianti DOCG must contain a minimum of _____ percent Sangiovese.

5. In addition to Sangiovese, what grapes are permitted to be used in basic Chianti?

   _____

   _____

6. What are the seven subzones of the Chianti DOCG? _____

   _____

   _____

   _____

7. Chianti Classico DOCG must contain a minimum of _____ percent Sangiovese.

8. What classification was approved by the Chianti Classico Consortium in 2014 for use with high-quality wines produced exclusively from estate-grown grapes?

   _____

9. Brunello di Montalcino DOCG must be aged for a minimum of _____ in wood and a minimum of _____ in the bottle. In addition, it may not be released before

   _____

10. Vin santo that is light red or amber in hue is sometimes referred to as _____

11. What is Tuscany's only white wine DOCG? _____

Match each of the following terms with its appropriate definition. Each term will be used only once.

Sangiovese	Governo	Tignanello	Morellino	Bolgheri
Canaiolo Nero	Vin Santo	Chianti Classico	Carmignano	
Colorino	Sassicaia	Vino Nobile	Prugnolo Gentile	

1. _____ The original Super Tuscan, produced by Tenuta San Guido

2. _____ Tuscan wine produced in and around the village of Montepulciano

3. _____ A Tuscan wine that must be produced using 10% to 20% Cabernet Sauvignon or Cabernet Franc

4. _____ The major red grape variety of Tuscany

5. _____ The term used for the Sangiovese grape variety in the region of Scansano

6. _____ An ancient winemaking technique that involves the addition of overripe grapes to a vat of new wine as it is finishing fermentation

7. _____ The historic heart of the Chianti region, dating back to the Middle Ages

8. _____ A type of sweet wine made in Tuscany (and other areas) using dried grapes and extensive aging

9. _____ Local name for the Sangiovese grape variety as it is used in Rosso di Montepulciano

10. _____ A red grape variety noted for its rich color and hearty tannins

11. _____ The town known as the birthplace of the Super Tuscan movement

12. _____ A red grape variety used widely throughout Tuscany as a blending partner for Sangiovese

13. _____ One of the earliest Super Tuscan-style wines, created by Marchese Piero Antinori

Using the map and the terms listed below, identify the wine-producing regions and cities in the Chianti region.

Colli Senesi	Pisa	Siena	Colli Aretini
Montespertoli	Greve	Colline Pisane	Montalbano
Chianti Classico	Florence	Colli Fiorentini	Rufina

Figure 10-4: Map Exercise – Chianti

1. _____

2. _____

3. _____

4. _____

5. _____

6. _____

7. _____

8. _____

9. _____

10. _____

11. _____

12. _____

Mark each of the following statements as true or false.

1. _____ Emilia-Romagna is a triangular-shaped region that stretches across the Italian Peninsula almost from one side to the other.

2. _____ Est! Est!! Est!!! is a well-known wine produced in Umbria.

3. _____ Romagna Albana DOCG (previously known as Albana di Romagna) was the first white wine to achieve the DOCG designation.

4. _____ Montepulciano d'Abruzzo DOC wines are made using a minimum of 85% Montepulciano grapes.

5. _____ Orvieto DOC is one of the leading white wines of Umbria.

6. _____ Frascati DOC is a red wine produced in the Lazio region.

7. _____ Torgiano Rosso Riserva is a DOCG wine produced in Modena.

8. _____ Castelli di Jesi Verdicchio Riserva DOCG is a crisp, dry white wine produced in the Marches region.

9. _____ Cònero DOCG, a red wine made using the Montepulciano and Sangiovese grape varieties, is produced in the Marches region.

10. _____ Most Lambrusco is produced in Emilia-Romagna; however, some is produced in Lombardy as well.

11. _____ Trebbiano d'Abruzzo is the leading red wine of the Abruzzo region.

12. _____ A semi-dry Orvieto may be labeled with the term *abboccato*.

13. _____ Cerasuolo d'Abruzzo DOC is a cherry-colored, lighter style of Montepulciano d'Abruzzo.

14. _____ Montefalco Sagrantino, made with 100% Sagrantino grapes, is a white wine produced in Umbria.

15. _____ There are four DOCs specifically for vin santo in Tuscany, including the Vin Santo del Chianti DOC.

Match each of the following terms with its appropriate definition. Each term will be used only once.

Taurasi   Sicily   Nero d'Avola   Primitivo
Negroamaro   Aglianico   Greco di Bianco   Grenache
Calabria   Campania   Vesuvio
Vermentino di Gallura   Cerasuolo di Vittoria   Cirò

1. _____ The only DOCG wine produced in Sicily

2. _____ Production zone for Lacryma Christi wines

3. _____ Region that can be described as the "toe of the boot" on Italy's peninsula

4. _____ Red grape variety used to produce a sweet, late-harvest DOCG wine in Manduria (Puglia)

5. _____ A boldly-flavored red DOCG wine produced in Campania

6. _____ DOC wine of Calabria; the red version is produced using the Gaglioppo grape variety

7. _____ Red grape variety used in the wines of the Salice Salentino DOC

8. _____ Dried-grape dessert wine produced in small amounts in Calabria

9. _____ Main grape variety used in the wines of the Cannonau di Sardegna DOC

10. _____ DOCG white wine produced on the island of Sardinia

11. _____ Island located just west of Calabria

12. _____ Main grape variety used in Cerasuolo di Vittoria

13. _____ Main grape variety used in Taurasi DOCG

14. _____ Wine region surrounding the town of Naples

Fill in the missing information regarding Marsala in the table below.

Marsala DOC	
Location	
Main Grape Varieties	
Three Main Types	

Sweetness Levels:	
Secco (dry)	
Semisecco (semidry)	
Dolce (sweet)	

Aging Requirements:	
Marsala Fine	
Marsala Superiore	
Marsala Superiore Riserva	
Marsala Vergine/Marsala Solera	
Marsala Vergine Stravecchio	

1. Which of the following is a white wine produced in Tuscany?
   a. Vernaccia di San Gimignano
   b. Morellino di Scansano
   c. Roero Arneis
   d. Orvieto

2. Which of the following grape varieties is used in the production of Gavi?
   a. Trebbiano Toscano
   b. Cortese
   c. Sangiovese
   d. Barbera

3. Which of the following terms was coined in the 1970s as a result of the strict Chianti DOC regulations in place at the time?
   a. Vin Santo
   b. Chianti Classico
   c. Super Tuscan
   d. Chianti Rufina

4. Which of the following wines is required to contain 10% to 20% Cabernet Sauvignon or Cabernet Franc?
   a. Vino Nobile di Montepulciano
   b. Super Tuscan
   c. Morellino di Scansano
   d. Carmignano

5. Chianti Classico must contain a minimum of _____ Sangiovese.
   a. 65%
   b. 75%
   c. 80%
   d. 85%

6. Which of the following phrases best describes Recioto di Soave?
   a. A dry white wine produced in Piedmont
   b. A sweet white wine produced in Piedmont
   c. A dry white wine produced in Veneto
   d. A sweet white wine produced in Veneto

7. Which of the following types of wines is produced in the DOCG surrounding the town of Asolo?
   a. Prosecco
   b. Bardolino
   c. Picolit
   d. Franciacorta

8. Which of the following wines is based on the Montepulciano grape variety?
   a. Sforzato
   b. Torgiano
   c. Cerasuolo d'Abruzzo
   d. Rosso di Montalcino

9. Which of the following wines must be made from 100% Nebbiolo grapes?
   a. Barolo and Barbaresco
   b. Barolo and Gattinara
   c. Barbaresco and Ghemme
   d. Barbaresco and Gattinara

10. Which of the following is a lightly sparkling wine produced in Piedmont?
    a. Prosecco
    b. Brachetto d'Acqui
    c. Grecco Bianco
    d. Fiano d'Avellino

11. Which of the following wines is made using the Aglianico grape variety?
    a. Rosso Conero
    b. Montefalco Sagrantino
    c. Taurasi
    d. Cannonau di Sardegna

12. Where is Marsala produced?
    a. Tuscany
    b. Sicily
    c. Umbria
    d. Calabria

13. Which of the following wine regions surrounds the city of Naples?
    a. Apulia
    b. Basilicata
    c. Calabria
    d. Campania

14. Which of the following is an alternative name often used for the Trentino-Alto Adige region?
    a. Suvereto
    b. Pavese
    c. Südtirol
    d. Cornia

15. Which of the following was the first white wine to achieve DOCG status in Italy?
    a. Romagna Albana
    b. Vermentino di Gallura
    c. Recioto di Soave
    d. Rosso Piceno

16. Castelli di Jesi Verdicchio Riserva DOCG is produced in which of the following regions?
    a. Campania
    b. Lazio
    c. Marches
    d. Lombardy

17. What are the main grape varieties used in the production of Orvieto?
    a. Sangiovese and Barbera
    b. Trebbiano Toscano and Grechetto
    c. Garganega and Sagrantino
    d. Primitivo and Aglianico

18. Which of the following wines is produced in Emilia-Romagna?
    a. Lambrusco
    b. Carmignano
    c. Prosecco
    d. Est! Est!! Est!!! di Montefiascone

19. What grape variety is used in the production of Salice Salentino?
    a. Montepulciano
    b. Primitivo
    c. Passerina
    d. Negroamaro

20. Which of the following wines is required to be produced using 100% Sangiovese?
    a. Vino Nobile di Montepulciano DOCG
    b. Carmignano DOCG
    c. Brunello di Montalcino DOCG
    d. Morellino di Scansano DOCG

21. Which of the following areas is located furthest south?
    a. Montalbano
    b. Colline Pisane
    c. Colli Senesi
    d. Barbera d'Asti

22. Which of the following DOCs extends from the Veneto and into Friuli-Venezia Giulia?
    a. Amarone della Valpolicella
    b. Lison-Pramaggiore
    c. Piave Malanotte
    d. Friuli Colli Orientali

SPAIN

LEARNING OBJECTIVES

After studying this chapter, the candidate should be able to:

- Identify the general role and position of Spain in the global wine industry.
- Recall the physical location and general climate of Spain's major wine regions.
- Recognize the hierarchy of Spanish wine designations.

- Describe the grape varieties and wine styles of Rioja, Sherry, and Cava.
- Recall the wine regions and major grapes of Galicia, the Duero Valley, Navarra, and Catalonia.
- Discuss the differences between the fino and oloroso production methods and styles for Sherry.

EXERCISE 1: SPANISH GRAPE VARIETIES: MATCHING

Match each of the following terms with its appropriate definition. Each term will be used only once.

Tinta Roriz	Cencibel	Macabeo	Albariño
Aragonêz	Monastrell	Airén	
Tinta del País	Ull de Llebre	Garnacha	

1. _____ Synonym for the Viura grape variety

2. _____ Synonym for Tempranillo used in Ribera del Duero

3. _____ Spanish term for Grenache

4. _____ Synonym for Tempranillo used in Portugal's Douro River Valley

5. _____ Spanish term for Mourvèdre

6. _____ Main grape variety used in Rías Baixas

7. _____ Synonym for Tempranillo used in Catalonia

8. _____ The most widely planted grape variety in Spain

9. _____ Synonym for Tempranillo used in much of Portugal

10. _____ Synonym for Tempranillo used in La Mancha

Using the map and the terms listed below, identify the following wine-producing areas of Spain.

Rías Baixas
Jumilla
La Mancha
Jerez-Xéres-Sherry
Terra Alta
Toro
Valencia

Somontano
Penedès
Tarragona
Rioja
Montsant
Yecla
Montilla-Moriles

Ribeiro
Cigales
Bixkaiko Txakolina
Rueda
Navarra
Costers del Segre
Bierzo

Priorat
Ribera del Duero
Valdepeñas
Ribeira Sacra
Málaga

1. _____

2. _____

3. _____

4. _____

5. _____

6. _____

7. _____

8. _____

9. _____

10. _____

11. _____

12. _____

Figure 11-1: Map Exercise – Spain

13. _____

14. _____

15. _____

16. _____

17. _____

18. _____

19. _____

20. _____

21. _____

22. _____

23. _____

24. _____

25. _____

26. _____

EXERCISE 3: SPANISH WINE LAWS: MATCHING

Using the following list of terms, insert the correct labels onto the Spanish Wine Law Pyramid.

Vinos de Pago   DO   Vinos de Calidad (VCIG)

DOCa   Wine   PGI

Vinos de la Tierra   Vinos de Mesa

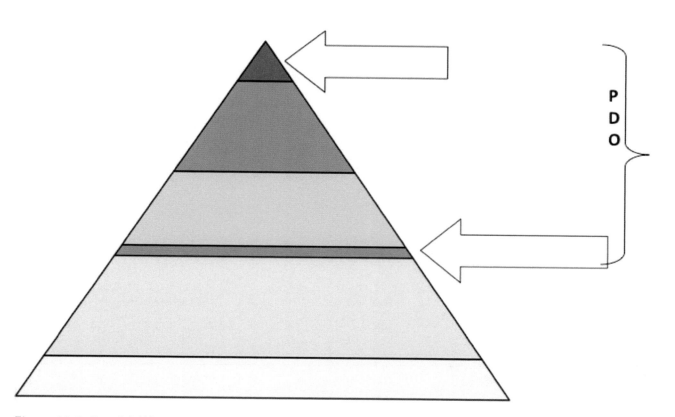

Figure 11-2: Spanish Wine Laws Exercise

Fill in the missing information regarding Spanish wine label laws in the table below.

Terms used by both PGI and PDO wines:	
	Wine that has spent a minimum of 18 months aging in barricas or in the bottle
	Wine that has spent a minimum of 24 months aging in barricas or in the bottle
	Wine that has spent a minimum of 36 months aging in a strongly oxidative environment and exposed to any combination of light, oxygen, and heat

Terms used by PDO wines only:				
	Red Wines		**White and Rosé Wines**	
Crianza	Barrel Aging:	Total Aging:	Barrel Aging:	Total Aging:
	Red Wines		**White and Rosé Wines**	
Reserva	Barrel Aging:	Total Aging:	Barrel Aging:	Total Aging:
	Red Wines		**White and Rosé Wines**	
Gran Reserva	Barrel Aging:	Total Aging:	Barrel Aging:	Total Aging:
	Term that may be used for PDO wine released the year after it was made, or aged for a shorter period of time than the minimum required for Crianza			

Match each of the following terms with its appropriate definition. Each term will be used only once.

Priorat	Navarra	Valdeorras	Catalonia	Rías Baixas
Rueda	Tarragona	Ribeiro	Cigales	Ribera del Duero
Montsant	Somontano	Penedès	Galicia	

1. _____ Located just to the west of Ribera del Duero, this DO is known mainly for reds and rosados based on the Tinta del Pais and Garnacha grape varieties

2. _____ This DO is well-known as one of the first areas in Spain to modernize wine production and was the first to use stainless steel temperature-controlled fermentation

3. _____ DO located in the foothills of the Pyrenees, within the region of Aragón

4. _____ The most famous of Galicia's wine regions, known for high-acid wines made from Albariño, Loureira, and Treixadura

5. _____ Region in Galicia known for its indigenous varieties of Godello and Mencia

6. _____ A well-known and established producer of white wines based on the Verdejo grape variety

7. _____ DO, located just to the north of the Rioja DO, historically known for rosados and currently expanding with international varieties

8. _____ DO located just to the east of Rías Baixas

9. _____ The only region of Spain to have a DO that covers the entire autonomous region

10. _____ DO famous for Garnacha-based wines and llicorella soils

11. _____ A small DO, created in 2001 and located adjacent to Priorat

12. _____ Area located in the northwest corner of Spain, exposed to the Atlantic Ocean, and often referred to as Green Spain

13. _____ Region in the Duero Valley with some of the highest-elevation vineyards in Spain

14. _____ Large DO located in Catalonia, just south of Penedès

Using numbers 1–8 and the terms below, identify the main cities in the Rioja region, and the provinces in and surrounding the Rioja region.

Navarra	La Rioja	Zaragoza	Soria
Burgos	Alava	Logroño	Haro

Figure 11-3: Map Exercise – the Rioja DOCa

1. _____

2. _____

3. _____

4. _____

5. _____

6. _____

7. _____

8. _____

9. _____

10. _____

11. _____

12. _____

13. _____

14. _____

Using numbers 9–11 and the terms below, identify the zones of the Rioja DOCa.

Rioja Oriental	Rioja Alta	Rioja Alavesa

15. _____

Using numbers 12–18 and the terms below, identify the river valleys of the Rioja region.

16. _____

Najerilla Valley	Cidacos Valley	Iregua Valley
Leza Valley	Alhama Valley	
Jubera Valley	Oja Valley	

17. _____

18. _____

EXERCISE 7: RIOJA: SHORT ANSWER/FILL IN THE BLANK

Fill in the blanks for the following statements or questions.

1. In the year _____, Rioja was the first region designated as a DO; in the year _____, it was the first region to be elevated to DOCa status as well.

2. The Rioja region lies in the _____ River Valley, mostly in the province of _____. About one-third of the vineyards are situated within the neighboring provinces of _____ and _____.

3. The _____ is the high-altitude, hilly subregion of Rioja located mainly south of the Ebro River.

4. The _____ is located on the western side of the Rioja area, north of the Ebro River.

5. The _____ is the flatter, eastern area of the Rioja.

6. Red varieties cover well over _____% of the vineyard area in Rioja.

7. _____ is the main red grape of the area, while other permitted red grapes include _____.

8. What is the principal grape variety used in white Rioja? _____.

9. Other indigenous white grapes used in white Rioja include _____. The international varieties _____ are now being planted as well.

10. Rioja's prominence is in part due to winemakers from _____ who settled in the region not long after phylloxera arrived in France.

11. Red Rioja is typically aged in barrels made of _____.

12. The long aging periods for red Rioja mean less of a focus on _____ flavors and more emphasis on _____.

13. Rioja Rosado is generally made from a blend of grapes dominated by the _____ grape variety.

14. Red Rioja DOCa using the Gran Reserva designation must age for a total of _____ months, to include a minimum of _____ months in the barrel and _____ months in the bottle.

Fill in the missing information regarding Cava in the table below.

CAVA	
Grape Varieties:	
	The three classic grape varieties used in Cava
	The same grape as Rioja's Viura, this grape produces dry wines of balanced acidity
	This grape forms the basis for most Cava blends as it provides a good deal of body and acidity
	This grape adapts well to higher-elevation vineyards and produces wines with great subtlety
	This international white grape variety has recently been added to the list of grapes allowed in Cava
	This red grape variety, thought to be native to Catalonia, is authorized for use in rosé (rosado) Cava only
	These three red grapes are also approved for use in Cava
Production Requirements:	
	Required method of production for all Cava
	Minimum lees aging time for basic Cava
	Required sweetness level for basic Cava
	Minimum lees aging time for Cava Reserva
	Required sweetness level for Cava Reserva
	Minimum lees aging time for Cava Gran Reserva
	Required sweetness level for Cava Gran Reserva
	Minimum lees aging time for Cava de Paraje Calificado
	Required sweetness level for Cava de Paraje Calificado

Match each of the following terms with its appropriate definition. Each term will be used only once.

Pale Cream   Albariza   Pedro Ximénez   Arena   Palo Cortado
Barro   Amontillado   Moscatel   Fino   Cream
Oloroso   Manzanilla   Palomino   Montilla-Moriles

1. _____   The general category of Sherries that undergo biological aging

2. _____   General category of Sherries that do not develop flor

3. _____   A type of fino Sherry that must be aged in Sanlúcar de Barrameda

4. _____   Type of sweetened fino Sherry originally made in Bristol

5. _____   Most widely grown grape variety in the Jerez DO

6. _____   Grape variety often used to add sweetness to some Sherries; also made
                               into a well-aged, very dark dried grape Sherry

7. _____   Grape used in small quantities to impart a "fruity" characteristic to
                               some Sherries

8. _____   White, chalky soil ideal for growing Palomino grapes

9. _____   Clay soil preferred by Pedro Ximénez grapes

10. _____   Sandy soil good for growing Moscatel grapes

11. _____   Wine region that lies to the east of Jerez, known for Sherry-style wines

12. _____   Style of Sherry that started as a fino but was subsequently aged
                               without flor

13. _____   A rare style of Sherry made from fino-quality wine that did not develop
                               flor as expected

14. _____   A sweetened oloroso Sherry

1. Which of the following grape varieties is a major component in the wines of Rías Baixas?
   a. Albariño
   b. Macabeo
   c. Verdejo
   d. Airén

2. Which of the following represents the three subregions of the Rioja region?
   a. Rioja Alta, Rioja Baja, and Rioja del Sur
   b. Rioja Alta, Rioja Norte, and Rioja Ebro
   c. Rioja Oriental, Rioja Ebro, and Rioja Alavesa
   d. Rioja Alta, Rioja Alavesa, and Rioja Oriental

3. What are the three classic grape varieties used in the production of Cava?
   a. Macabeo, Verdejo, and Pinot Noir
   b. Parellada, Macabeo, and Verdejo
   c. Xarel-lo, Pinot Noir, and Macabeo
   d. Macabeo, Parellada, and Xarel-lo

4. Which of the following wine regions specializes in crisp white wines based on the Verdejo grape variety?
   a. Priorat
   b. Ribeira Sacra
   c. Rueda
   d. Jerez

5. What is the minimum lees aging time required for Cava de Paraje Calificado?
   a. 36 months
   b. 24 months
   c. 60 months
   d. There is no minimum

6. Which of the following wine regions is a DOCa known for its llicorella soils?
   a. Ribera del Duero
   b. Priorat
   c. Navarra
   d. Málaga

7. What is the main grape variety used in white Rioja?
   a. Palomino
   b. Garnacha Blanca
   c. Viura
   d. Malvasia

8. What is the most widely grown grape variety in Spain?
   a. Airén
   b. Tempranillo
   c. Garnacha
   d. Macabeo

9. Which of the following grapes is often used as a sweetening agent in Sherry?
   a. Garnacha
   b. Tinta Roriz
   c. Pedro Ximénez
   d. Tinta del Toro

10. What are the three main soils in the region of Jerez?
    a. Albariza, Barro, and Clay
    b. Barro, Arena, and Albariza
    c. Arena, Llicorella, and Barro
    d. Llicorella, Albariza, and Arena

11. Which of the following aging terms may be used for PDO wines that are released the year after harvest?
    a. Joven
    b. Tipica
    c. Pago
    d. Calificado

12. How much total aging time is required for a typical Spanish red wine labeled as a Crianza?
    a. Six months
    b. One year
    c. Eighteen months
    d. Two years

13. How does the Crianza aging requirement for red Rioja differ from that of other Spanish red wines?
    a. Red Rioja requires more time in wood than other red wines.
    b. Red Rioja requires less time in wood than other red wines.
    c. Red Rioja must spend the entire length of the required aging time in wood.
    d. Red Rioja must be fermented in new oak barrels in order to use the term "Crianza."

14. How much total aging time is required for a typical Spanish red wine labeled as a Reserva?
    a. Two years
    b. Three years
    c. Four years
    d. Five years

15. How much total aging time is required for a typical Spanish red wine labeled as a Gran Reserva?
    a. Two years
    b. Three years
    c. Four years
    d. Five years

16. Which of the following wine regions is located just to the northeast of the Rioja DOCa?
    a. Ribera del Duero
    b. Penedès
    c. Navarra
    d. Jumilla

17. The Somontano DO is located within which of the following autonomous regions?
    a. Catalonia
    b. Aragón
    c. Castilla-La Mancha
    d. La Rioja

18. Which of the following DOs is nearly surrounded by the larger La Mancha DO?
    a. Valdepeñas
    b. Yecla
    c. Toro
    d. Valdeorras

PORTUGAL

CHAPTER TWELVE

LEARNING OBJECTIVES

After studying this chapter, the candidate should be able to:

- Identify the physical location and general climate of Portugal's major wine regions.
- Recognize the hierarchy of wine designations from Vinho de Portugal to DOC.
- Describe the major grape varieties and wine styles of Port and Madeira.
- Recall significant DOCs for unfortified wine and their primary grape varieties.

EXERCISE 1: PORTUGUESE GRAPE VARIETIES: MATCHING

Match each of the following terms with its appropriate definition. Each term will be used only once.

Tinta Roriz	Gouveio	Alvarinho	Touriga Franca	Trincadeira
Baga	Fernão Pires	Malvasia	Touriga Nacional	Castelão

1. _____ One of the primary red grapes used in Port; provides firm structure and black-fruit flavors

2. _____ Red grape variety sometimes referred to as Periquita

3. _____ Portugal's most widely grown white grape variety

4. _____ White grape variety grown in the Vinho Verde region; also the star of Spain's Rías Baixas DO

5. _____ White grape variety used in a sweet style of Madeira, where it is sometimes referred to as Malmsey

6. _____ Red grape variety also known as Tempranillo

7. _____ Red grape variety also known as Tinta Amarela

8. _____ One of the predominant white grape varieties used in white Port

9. _____ One of the primary red grape varieties used in Port; lends floral notes to the blend

10. _____ Highly tannic red grape variety; often used in the red wines of the Bairrada DOC

Using the map and the terms listed below, identify the regional wine designations of Portugal.

Alentejano   Península de Setúbal   Terras do Dão   Minho
Lisboa   Beira Atlântico   Algarve   Duriense
Tejo   Transmontano   Terras da Beira   Terras de Cister

Map Exercise: Mainland Portugal

Copyright: The Society of Wine Educators 2016

Figure 12-1: Map Exercise – Mainland Portugal

1. _____

2. _____

3. _____

4. _____

5. _____

6. _____

7. _____

8. _____

9. _____

10. _____

11. _____

12. _____

EXERCISE 3: PORTUGUESE WINE REGIONS: SHORT ANSWER/FILL IN THE BLANK

Fill in the blanks or give a short answer for the following statements or questions.

1. Vinho Verde is produced in the _____ region under the _____ DOC.

2. The two main grape varieties used in white Vinho Verde are _____ _____ .

3. Red Vinho Verde is made primarily from the _____ grape variety.

4. Unfortified wines produced in the Douro River Valley from traditional Port grape varieties are categorized as _____ .

5. Unfortified wines produced in the Douro River Valley from international grape varieties such as Cabernet Sauvignon are categorized as _____ .

6. The Baga grape is used to make highly tannic red wines under the _____ DOC, located within the Beiras VR.

7. The _____ DOC, located just south of the Minho region, produces many styles of wine but focuses on _____ .

8. The Península de Setúbal is home to a well-known, sweet wine produced from the Muscat grape, known as _____ .

9. _____ is the southernmost Portuguese wine region on the mainland.

10. The _____ region is located on a chain of nine islands approximately 1,000 miles off the west coast of Portugal. Three islands, _____ _____ _____ , have their own DOCs.

11. The small DOC of _____ , located near the famous surfing beach of Guincho, is famous for vineyards planted in the sand.

12. The _____ DOC is located within the Península de Setúbal region and produces mainly red wines based on the _____ grape variety.

Using numbers 1–3 and the terms below, identify the three main subregions of the Douro.

Cima Corgo   Baixa Corgo   Douro Superior

Figure 12-2: Map Exercise – Subzones of the Douro DOC

1. _____

2. _____

3. _____

4. _____

5. _____

6. _____

7. _____

8. _____

9. _____

10. _____

11. _____

12. _____

Using numbers 4–12 and the terms listed below, identify the main towns and municipalities located within the Douro.

Pinhão	Sabrosa	Tua
Régua	Vila Nova de Foz Côa	Vila Real
Torre de Moncorvo	Armamar	Lamego

Fill in the missing information regarding Port in the table below.

PORT	
Region of origin:	
Subregions:	
GRAPE VARIETIES:	
Five preferred red grape varieties:	
Two predominant white grape varieties:	
STYLES OF PORT:	
	The simplest style of Port; aged in large oak vats for about two years before being bottled and ready-to-drink
	Wine from a single year, matured in large oak casks for four to six years after harvest
	Port that has been aged in oak for a minimum of seven years before bottling
	Wine from a single year designated as being an outstanding year; aged for two to three years in cask before being bottled
	Port produced from the grapes of one year and one estate
	A single-vintage tawny Port
	Port produced using Malvasia Fina and Gouveio grapes, among others
	Non-traditional style of Port originally produced by Croft, first released in 2008

Fill in the blanks or give a short answer for the following statements or questions.

1. Madeira is produced on an island located in the _____ Ocean, approximately _____ miles off the coast of Morocco.

2. All fortified wine produced on the island is categorized as _____.

3. Unfortified table wines produced on the island are considered *Vinho Regional* and are categorized as _____.

4. The most widely planted grape on the island is _____.

5. The four noble grapes of Madeira are _____
_____.

6. Madeira can be made in both dry and sweet styles, depending on whether the wine is _____ _____ during fermentation or after.

7. The dry styles of Madeira are made from _____ grapes.

8. The sweet styles of Madeira are made from _____ grapes.

9. In the _____ method of production, Madeira is stored in the rafters of a warm building and allowed to age for several years.

10. In the _____ method of production, Madeira is left in a concrete or stainless steel vat and heated via hot water for several months.

11. The finest Madeiras are made using the _____ method.

12. The four styles of Madeira are described as:

Sercial: _____

Verdelho: _____

Boal: _____

Malmsey: _____

1. Which of the following grape varieties is known for providing Port with a firm structure and black-fruit flavors?
   a. Tinta Roriz
   b. Trincadeira
   c. Touriga Franca
   d. Touriga Nacional

2. Which of the following grape varieties is known for providing Port with floral and blackberry notes?
   a. Tinta Roriz
   b. Trincadeira
   c. Touriga Franca
   d. Touriga Nacional

3. Which of the following grape varieties is also known as Tempranillo?
   a. Baga
   b. Castelão
   c. Tinta Roriz
   d. Tinta Cão

4. Vinho Verde is produced in which of the following regions?
   a. The Minho
   b. Algarve
   c. Alentejano
   d. The Dão

5. What are the three subregions of the Douro Valley?
   a. Baixo Corgo, Baixo Superior, and Douro Baja
   b. Douro Superior, Douro Alta, and Cima Corgo
   d. Douro Duriense, Cima Corgo, and Baixo Corgo
   d. Cima Corgo, Baixo Corgo, and Douro Superior

6. Which of the following properly lists the traditional styles of Madeira, in order from driest to sweetest?
   a. Sercial, Verdelho, Boal, Malmsey
   b. Malmsey, Boal, Sercial, Verdelho
   c. Boal, Verdelho, Malmsey, Sercial
   d. Verdelho, Sercial, Boal, Malmsey

7. Which of the following styles of Port, considered to be the simplest style, is aged in large oak vats for two years before being bottled and ready-to-drink?
   a. Tawny Port
   b. Ruby Port
   c. Vintage Port
   d. Fino Port

8. Which of the following is a single-vintage tawny Port?
   a. Late-Bottled Vintage Port
   b. Primo Port
   c. Colheita Port
   d. Single Quinta Port

9. What style of Port is produced using wine from a single year, matured in large oak casks for four to six years after harvest?
   a. Vintage Port
   b. Ruby Port
   c. Colheita Port
   d. Late-Bottled Vintage Port

10. Which of the following island chains produces wine about 1,000 miles off the west coast of Portugal?
    a. The Canary Islands
    b. The Azores
    c. The Gulf Islands
    d. The Ionian Islands

11. The Baga grape variety is known for which of the following properties?
    a. High tannin
    b. Deep yellow color
    c. Low acid
    d. Being seedless

12. The region of Setúbal is known for which of the following wines?
    a. Baga de Arrábida
    b. Fernão Pires de Península
    c. Moscatel de Setúbal
    d. Lagos de Setúbal

GERMANY

LEARNING OBJECTIVES

After studying this chapter, the candidate should be able to:

- Discuss the general role and position of Germany in the global wine industry.
- Recall the physical location and general climate of Germany's major wine regions.
- Recognize the importance of Riesling to the German wine industry.

- Understand the hierarchy of wine designations from Wein to Prädikatswein, along with the progression of Prädikat levels from Kabinett to Trockenbeerenauslese.
- Discuss the differences among Anbaugebiete, Bereiche, Grosslagen, and Einzellagen.
- Identify the grape varieties and wine styles of the key wine regions of Germany.

EXERCISE 1: GERMANY: MAP EXERCISE

Using numbers 1–6 and the terms listed below, identify the following German cities.

| Berlin | Munich | Hamburg |
| Hanover | Cologne | Leipzig |

1. _____

2. _____

3. _____

4. _____

5. _____

6. _____

Figure 13-1: Map Exercise – Germany

Figure 13-1: Map Exercise – Germany

Using numbers 7–19 and the terms listed below, identify the location of the 13 main wine regions of Germany.

Rheinhessen	Franken	Saale-Unstrut
Sachsen	Nahe	Mosel
Baden	Pfalz	Hessische Bergstrasse
Württemberg	Rheingau	
Ahr	Mittelrhein	

7. _____

8. _____

9. _____

10. _____

11. _____

12. _____

13. _____

14. _____

15. _____

16. _____

17. _____

18. _____

19. _____

Match each of the following terms with its appropriate definition. Each term will be used only once.

Geschützte Ursprungsbezeichnung (gU)

Edelfäule

Prädikatswein

Wein

Geschützte Geographische Angabe (ggA)

Trocken

Grauburgunder

Halbtrocken

Qualitätswein

Weissburgunder

Deutscher Wein

Oechsle

Spätburgunder

Riesling

1. _____ German name for Pinot Gris

2. _____ German name for Pinot Blanc

3. _____ Most widely planted red grape in Germany

4. _____ A German table wine made from 100% German grapes

5. _____ A German table wine that may be produced from imported bulk wine

6. _____ Most widely planted grape in Germany

7. _____ German wine category that contains what used to be referred to as "Landwein"

8. _____ Term used for dry German wines

9. _____ Term used for off-dry German wines

10. _____ Term used to denote all German PDO wines

11. _____ Category of German PDO wines that allows for chaptalization

12. _____ Category of German PDO wines that does not allow chaptalization

13. _____ German term for botrytis

14. _____ The name of the system used in Germany to determine sugar ripeness in grapes

Fill in the blanks with the appropriate term for the subcategories of Prädikatswein, listed in ascending order of grape ripeness.

1. _____ The lowest ripeness level of the German Prädikat

2. _____ Wines of additional ripeness made from grapes picked after a designated date; translates as "late harvest"

3. _____ Translating as "selected harvest," these wines are made from grapes that have reached a required level of sugar

4. _____ Translating as "selected berries," these are sweet wines that may be affected by botrytis

5. _____ Wines made from frozen grapes that must be harvested at the same level of ripeness as the previous category

6. _____ Wines made from individually picked, overripe berries that are often affected by botrytis

Fill in the blanks with the appropriate term for the geographical indications for German wines, listed in order from largest to smallest.

1. _____ Germany has 13 of these designated wine regions.

2. _____ Equal to regional or district appellations, Germany has approximately 40 of these designated areas.

3. _____ Equivalent to a large grouping of closely located vineyards, approximately 160 of these designated areas exist in Germany.

4. _____ This area may contain a single vineyard or a small group of vineyards. There are approximately 2,700 of these areas in Germany.

Match each of the following terms with its appropriate definition. Each term will be used only once.

Verband Deutscher Prädikatsweingüter (VDP)   Feinherb   Grosses Gewächs
Lieblich   Gutsabfüllung   Abfüller
Süssreserve   Grosse Lage   Erste Lage
Weissherbst   Sekt   Trocken
Erzeugerabfüllung   Chaptalization   Schaumwein

1. _____   An organization of German wine estates committed to terroir-driven viticulture

2. _____   A term used to indicate that a wine was made from the highest-level vineyards of an estate

3. _____   A term used to indicate that a wine is made from the second-highest-level vineyards of an estate

4. _____   Unfermented grape juice that is sometimes used to increase the sweetness in a wine

5. _____   Label term used to indicate an estate-bottled wine

6. _____   Label term that indicates a producer-bottled wine made by grower cooperatives

7. _____   Label term that indicates a wine produced by a commercial winery from purchased grapes

8. _____   Label term that while legally undefined, generally refers to an off-dry wine

9. _____   Label term that indicates a semi-sweet wine

10. _____   Label term that typically refers to a wine with a sugar level of 9g/L or less

11. _____   Label term that may be used on a dry wine produced from a VDP Grosse Lage vineyard

12. _____   German sparkling wine produced via carbonation

13. _____   The practice of adding sugar to must before fermentation

14. _____   A German rosé of at least Qualitätswein quality made from a single variety

15. _____   German sparkling wine typically produced via the tank method

Match each of the following terms with its appropriate definition. Each term may be used more than once.

Baden	Sachsen	Württemberg	Rheingau	Rheinhessen
Pfalz	Ahr	Mosel	Franken	

1. _____ This small area produces only 2% of Germany's wines, yet its wines enjoy an excellent reputation

2. _____ One of the wine regions located in the former East Germany

3. _____ The largest wine region of Germany in terms of both area under vine and wine production

4. _____ The largest wine region of Germany in terms of ground area; however, only a small portion of the area is planted with grapes

5. _____ Has over 85% of its vines planted to red grapes, despite its northerly location

6. _____ Region known for blue slate soils and excellent Riesling

7. _____ This region is home to the well-known Bereich of Johannisberg

8. _____ Wine region that lies west of the Rhine River, with its southern edge stretching almost to Alsace

9. _____ Region with the most Einzellagen (over 500)

10. _____ Region with most of its vines planted along the Neckar River and in the Neckar River Valley

11. _____ Region near the city of Wiesbaden known for red slate soils

12. _____ Region that is home to six Bereiche, including Bernkastel, Saar, and Ruwertal

13. _____ This region is sometimes referred to as Palatinate

14. _____ The regional home of the Kaiserstuhl Bereich, noted for its warm weather

15. _____ Wines from this region are often packaged in a flask-shaped Bocksbeutel

1. Which of the following grapes is known in Germany as Grauburgunder?
   a. Riesling
   b. Pinot Gris
   c. Pinot Blanc
   d. Chardonnay

2. What is the most widely planted white grape variety in Germany?
   a. Riesling
   b. Müller-Thurgau
   c. Silvaner
   d. Grauburgunder

3. What is the most widely planted red grape variety in Germany?
   a. Pinot Noir
   b. Merlot
   c. Dornfelder
   d. St. Laurent

4. Which of the following German wine regions is located in the former East Germany?
   a. Mittelrhein
   b. Pfalz
   c. Sachsen
   d. Baden

5. Which of the following German wine regions is located farthest north?
   a. Baden
   b. Württemberg
   c. Franken
   d. Ahr

6. Which of the following grapes is known in Germany as Weissburgunder?
   a. Pinot Noir
   b. Pinot Blanc
   c. Silvaner
   d. Chardonnay

7. In the context of the German wine industry, which of the following terms refers to the most specific area?
   a. Anbaugebiet
   b. Grosslage
   c. Bereich
   d. Einzellage

8. What is Sekt?
   a. An off-dry German rosé
   b. A German sparkling wine
   c. A dry white wine produced using a blend of grape varieties
   d. A term used to refer to a co-operatively run wine estate

9. Of the following list of terms, which indicates the highest level of ripeness?
   a. Beerenauslese
   b. Kabinett
   c. Spätlese
   d. Auslese

10. Which of the following terms represents the highest classification of quality German wines?
    a. ggA (geschützte geographische Angabe)
    b. Gutswein
    c. Prädikatswein
    d. Deutscher Wein

11. What scale is used in Germany to measure grape density and ripeness?
    a. Brix
    b. Feinherb
    c. Abfüller
    d. Oechsle

12. Which of the following terms is used by the members of the VDP (Verband Deutscher Prädikatsweingüter) to indicate that the wine was made from the highest-level vineyards of an estate?
    a. Grosse Lage
    b. Erste Lage
    c. Charta
    d. Selection

13. Which of the following terms is used to refer to the 13 designated wine regions in Germany?
    a. Grosslagen
    b. Anbaugebiete
    c. Einzellagen
    d. Bereiche

14. Which of the following German wine regions is the largest, both in terms of area under vine and wine production?
    a. Rheinhessen
    b. Baden
    c. Ahr
    d. Mosel

15. Which of the following German wine regions is largely planted to red grapes?
    a. Mosel
    b. Hessische Bergstrasse
    c. Württemberg
    d. Mittelrhein

16. Where is the Mittelrhein area located?
    a. Downriver (north) of the Rheingau
    b. Upriver (south) of the Pfalz
    c. East of Sachsen
    d. North of Berlin

17. Which of the following is the easternmost wine region of the former West Germany?
    a. Nahe
    b. Rheingau
    c. Ahr
    d. Franken

18. Which of the following wine regions is located just above the northern edge of Baden?
    a. Saale-Unstrut
    b. Mosel
    c. Hessische Bergstrasse
    d. Württemberg

LEARNING OBJECTIVES

After studying this chapter, the candidate should be able to:

- Discuss the physical location and general climate of Austria's major wine regions.
- Recognize Austria's signature grape variety and other important grapes.
- Describe Austrian wine law and the hierarchy of Austrian wine designations.
- Discuss the other main wines and wine regions of central and eastern Europe.

EXERCISE 1: AUSTRIA: MAP EXERCISE

Using the map and the terms listed below, identify the regional wine designations of Austria.

Kamptal DAC   Wagram   Rosalia DAC   Kremstal DAC
Carnuntum DAC   Mittelburgenland DAC   Traisental DAC   Leithaberg DAC
Wachau   Weinviertel DAC   Thermenregion   Eisenberg DAC
Neusiedlersee DAC   Südsteiermark DAC   Wiener Gemischter Satz DAC
Weststeiermark DAC   Vulkanland Steiermark DAC

Map Exercise - Austria

Copyright: The Society of Wine Educators 2019

Figure 14-1: Map Exercise – Austria

1. _____
2. _____
3. _____
4. _____
5. _____
6. _____
7. _____
8. _____
9. _____
10. _____
11. _____
12. _____
13. _____
14. _____
15. _____
16. _____
17. _____

Fill in the blanks or give a short answer for the following statements or questions.

1. What percentage of Austria's wine production is white wine? _____

2. What portion of Austria's vineyards are planted with Grüner Veltliner? _____

3. What are some typical descriptors used for a young white wine made with Grüner Veltliner?

    _____

4. What grape is a cross between Riesling and Madeleine Royale?

    _____

5. In Austria, what alternative name is often used for Chardonnay? _____

6. What is the most widely planted red grape in Austria? _____

7. What red grape is also known as Lemberger or Kékfrankos?

    _____

8. What scale is used to measure must weight in Austria? _____

9. What terms may be used for an Austrian wine produced using dried grapes?

    _____

10. What is the lowest level on the Austrian Prädikat, and how does this differ from Germany's Prädikat system?

    _____

    _____

    _____

11. Austria has _____ grape varieties authorized for use in wines at the Qualitätswein and Prädikatswein level.
    Of these, _____ are red varieties and _____ are white.

12. Many of Austria's quality wine subregions are classified as _____ and
    have strict AOC-style regulations as to what type and styles of wine may be produced using the classification title.

Fill in the blanks or give a short answer for the following statements or questions.

1. _____ is the largest wine region (Weinbaugebiete) in Austria in terms of both geographical area and vineyard plantings.

2. The wines of the Weinviertel DAC are produced using 100% _____ _____ grapes.

3. The Mittelburgenland DAC produces red wines based on the _____ _____ grape variety.

4. The term *Ausbruch* is only allowed to be used in conjunction with the wine known as _____, which is produced near Lake _____ in the region of _____.

5. The Neusiedlersee DAC produces red wines based on the _____ grape variety.

6. _____ Veltliner is a pink-skinned grape grown in the Wagram area.

7. Wine taverns known as _____ are popular in and around the vineyards of Vienna.

8. The DAC that surrounds the city of Vienna is known as the _____ _____ .

9. The _____ DAC, located to the west of Lake Neusiedl, produces single-varietal white wines, blended white wines, and red wines based on the Blaufränkisch grape.

10. The _____ DAC is known for its volcanic soils.

11. The _____ DAC is known for the production of Schilcher rosé.

12. The city of Vienna lies on the _____ River.

13. What is the largest subregion of the Niederösterreich region? _____.

14. What is the westernmost subregion of the Niederösterreich region? _____.

15. The Schilcher grape variety is also known as _____.

Match each of the following terms with its appropriate definition. Each term will be used only once.

Rkatsiteli	Bulgaria	Chasselas	Rubin	Tribidrag
Kvevri	Saperavi	Slovenia	Tokaji Aszú	Graševina
Romania	Egri Bikavér	Croatia	Kékfrankos	Crimea

1. _____ The leading red grape of the Republic of Georgia

2. _____ Alternative name used for the Blaufränkisch grape variety

3. _____ The leading white grape variety of Switzerland

4. _____ A dessert wine produced in northern Hungary

5. _____ A Hungarian red wine traditionally known as Bull's Blood

6. _____ Half of this country's wine is produced in the Podravje region

7. _____ Country with many vineyard areas interspersed among islands and inlets formed by the Kvarner Gulf

8. _____ A grape variety known to be a Nebbiolo X Syrah cross

9. _____ An egg-shaped, earthenware vessel traditionally used in the Republic of Georgia

10. _____ Home of the Novy Svet Winery

11. _____ The predominant white grape variety of Eastern Europe

12. _____ The native Fetească Neagră grape is considered to be the flagship red variety of this country

13. _____ White grape variety also known as Welschriesling

14. _____ Country located to the south of (and across the Danube River from) Romania

15. _____ Grape variety also known as Crljenak Kaštelanski, Zinfandel, or Primitivo

1. Which of the following grape varieties is sometimes known as Morillon?
   a. Zinfandel
   b. Chasselas
   c. Riesling
   d. Chardonnay

2. What is the most widely planted red grape variety in Austria?
   a. Pinot Noir
   b. Zweigelt
   c. St. Laurent
   d. Merlot

3. Which of the following is a requirement of Bergwein?
   a. The grapes are grown on steeply-graded mountain slopes.
   b. The wine is produced using a field blend of at least four grape varieties.
   c. The wine is produced using partially botrytis-affected grapes.
   d. The wine is produced from grapes that are allowed to dry for 3 months after harvest.

4. A wine with the term *Federspiel* on the label is most likely from which of the following regions?
   a. Vienna
   b. Leithaberg
   c. The Wachau
   d. The Mosel

5. Which of the following is an Austrian DAC approved for both Riesling and Grüner Veltliner?
   a. Mittelrhein
   b. Kremstal
   c. Weinviertel
   d. Eisenberg

6. Which of the following is an Austrian DAC approved for red grapes only?
   a. Neusiedlersee
   b. Traisental
   c. Kamptal
   d. Leithaberg

7. Where is Egri Bikavér produced?
   a. Croatia
   b. Romania
   c. Austria
   d. Hungary

8. Which of the following countries is not a member of the European Union?
   a. Switzerland
   b. Croatia
   c. Austria
   d. Romania

9. What is the leading white grape variety of Switzerland?
   a. Rkatsiteli
   b. Tarnave
   c. Chasselas
   d. Airén

10. Which of the following grape varieties is also known as Fendant?
    a. Chardonnay
    b. Chasselas
    c. Pinot Noir
    d. Muscat

11. Which of the following is the most widely grown white grape variety in Georgia?
    a. Fetească Alba
    b. Saperavi
    c. Rkatsiteli
    d. Steinfeder

12. Which of the following is true concerning the wine industry of Croatia?
    a. Over 80% of the wine produced is red wine.
    b. The wine country is divided into three broad regions.
    c. The majority of the high-quality wine is produced in the inland region.
    d. The most widely grown grape variety is Graševina.

EASTERN MEDITERRANEAN

CHAPTER FIFTEEN

LEARNING OBJECTIVES

After studying this chapter, the candidate should be able to:

- Identify the physical location and general climate of Greece's major wine regions.
- Understand the hierarchy of wine designations used in Greece.
- Recognize significant appellations in Greece and their primary grape varieties.
- Describe the style and source of Commandaria.
- Understand the general status of the Israeli wine industry.

EXERCISE 1: GREECE: MAP EXERCISE

Using numbers 1 through 7 and the terms listed below, identify the major administrative regions of Greece.

Thessalia
Crete
Central Greece
Macedonia
Thrace
Epirus
Peloponnese

1. _____
2. _____
3. _____
4. _____
5. _____
6. _____
7. _____

Figure 15-1: Map Exercise – Greece

Using numbers 8 – 22 and the terms listed below, identify the following Greek wine-producing areas.

Figure 15-1: Map Exercise – Greece

Slopes of Meliton PDO
Muscat of Rio Patras PDO
Mavrodaphne of Cephalonia PDO
Mantinia PDO
Naoussa PDO
Rapsani PDO
Rhodes PDO
Malvasia Sitia PDO
Goumenissa PDO
Santorini PDO
Samos PDO
Amynteo PDO
Nemea PDO
Paros PDO
Muscat of Patras PDO

8. _____

9. _____

10. _____

11. _____

12. _____

13. _____

14. _____

15. _____

16. _____

17. _____

18. _____

19. _____

20. _____

21. _____

22. _____

Match each of the following terms with its appropriate definition. Each term will be used only once.

Onomasía Proeléfseos Anotéras Piótitos (OPAP)
Topikos Oínos (TO)
Assyrtiko
Kava
Agiorgitiko
Onomasía Proeléfseos Eleghoméni (OPE)
Roditis
Mavrodaphne

Xinomavro
Onomasía Katá Parádosi (OKP)
Verdea
Moschofilero
Epitrapézios Oínos (EO)
Muscat
Vinsanto

1. _____ Red grape variety used to produce a fortified wine on the island of Patras

2. _____ Term that indicates a PGI wine with oak aging

3. _____ Dessert wine specialty of Santorini

4. _____ Greek term for regional, PGI-level wine

5. _____ Classification of Greek wine used for traditional wines such as Retsina

6. _____ Top quality designation for Greek wines; used exclusively for sweet wines

7. _____ A pink-skinned grape variety native to the Peloponnese

8. _____ Red grape variety often compared to Pinot Noir and grown throughout northern Greece

9. _____ Top quality designation used for dry, unfortified wines

10. _____ High-acid white wine grape variety originally from Santorini

11. _____ A traditional, oxidative white wine

12. _____ Red grape variety grown mainly in the Peloponnese

13. _____ Classification for standard Greek table wine

14. _____ White grape variety used to produce sweet wines in many parts of Greece

15. _____ White grape variety used to produce dry wines in the Patras OPAP

Fill in the blanks or give a short answer for the following statements or questions.

1. A red PDO wine from Greece may be labeled with the term *reserve* if it is aged for a minimum of
_____ years, including at least _____ in oak.

2. A red PDO wine from Greece may be labeled with the term *grand reserve* if it is aged for a minimum of
_____ years, including at least _____ in oak.

3. A white or rosé PDO wine from Greece may be labeled with the term *reserve* if it is aged for a minimum of
_____ months in oak, with another _____ months in the bottle.

4. A white or rosé PDO wine from Greece may be labeled with the term *grand reserve* if it is aged for a
minimum of _____ years, including a minimum of _____ in oak.

5. The Greek term *palaiomenos se vareli* means _____ and may
be used for Greek wines that have _____ the minimum
requirements for oak aging.

6. What is the largest red wine appellation in Greece? _____

7. Where is Commandaria produced? _____

8. What are the two main grapes used in the production of Commandaria? _____
_____

9. What is the name of the traditional aging system used in the production of Commandaria?
_____

10. Most of the vineyards in Lebanon are located in the _____.

11. _____ is the leading wine producer in Lebanon.

12. The most important wine-producing region in Israel is _____, located in
the north of the country.

13. The _____ region of Israel is located in the southern part of the country, in a
semi-arid desert region.

14. The Israeli region of _____ is located between the Judean Hills and the
Coastal Plain.

15. The Israeli region of _____ includes the Sharon Plain.

1. Shomron, Shimson, and Negev are three of the main wine-producing regions in which of the following countries?
   a. Greece
   b. Cyprus
   c. Israel
   d. Lebanon

2. Which of the following is the largest red wine appellation in Greece?
   a. Santorini
   b. Rhodes
   c. Samos
   d. Nemea

3. Which of the following areas is located farthest north?
   a. Naoussa PDO
   b. Samos PDO
   c. Patras PDO
   d. Nemea PDO

4. Which of the following is a sweet wine produced on the island of Santorini?
   a. Kava
   b. Rasteau
   c. Vinsanto
   d. Patras

5. Which of the following is a red grape variety?
   a. Moschofilero
   b. Xinomavro
   c. Assyritiko
   d. Roditis

6. The Onomasía Katá Parádosi (OKP) classification is a special subcategory designed to protect which of the following wines?
   a. Commandaria
   b. Vinsanto
   c. Retsina
   d. Kava

7. Which of the following is a pink-skinned grape, widely grown in the Peloponnese?
   a. Mavrodaphne
   b. Assyritiko
   c. Agiorgitiko
   d. Moschofilero

8. The Bekaa Valley is one of the leading wine-producing regions of which of the following countries?
   a. Lebanon
   b. Greece
   c. Israel
   d. Turkey

9. Which of the following areas is located farthest south?
   a. Rapsani PDO
   b. Muscat of Rhodes PDO
   c. Slopes of Meliton PDO
   d. Muscat of Rio Patras PDO

10. Which of the following best describes Commandaria?
    a. An amber-colored dessert wine
    b. A dry white wine
    c. A sparkling red wine
    d. A red wine flavored with pine resin

LEARNING OBJECTIVES

After studying this chapter, the candidate should be able to:

- Identify the general role and position of the United States in the global wine industry.
- Understand the structure of the US wine industry, especially the three-tier system.
- Describe the differences between native American grapes, French-American hybrids, and vinifera.
- Discuss the differences between American viticultural areas and European appellations.
- Recall the major required and optional elements of a wine label in the United States.
- Recall the minimum content requirements for the use of place-of-origin terms, vintage dates, and grape variety names on a US wine label.
- Recognize the importance of California to the US wine industry.
- Identify the primary appellations, climatic zones, and major grapes of California, Washington, Oregon, and New York.
- Discuss the major wine-producing regions of Canada and Mexico.

EXERCISE 1: US WINE HISTORY: SHORT ANSWER/FILL IN THE BLANK

Fill in the blanks or give a short answer for the following statements or questions.

1. During what years was Prohibition in effect in the United States? _____

2. What 1849 event led to an increase in the population in California and, eventually, to an increased demand for California wine? _____

3. What 1976 event is considered the "turning point" that changed the world's perception of California wines?

   _____

   _____

4. Who is recognized for bringing European vines to Sonoma in 1861?_____

5. Who is recognized as the founder of the first Napa Valley winery in 1861? _____

6. Who was the founder of the first successful commercial winery in the United States (in Ohio)?_____

7. Who is André Tchelistcheff? _____

Match each of the following terms with its appropriate definition. Each term may be used more than once.

Producers   Off-premise retailers   ATF

Distributors   On-premise retailers   TTB

1. _____   Wine shops, liquor stores, and supermarkets

2. _____   Federal agency responsible for enforcing laws relevant to businesses engaged in the importation of alcohol

3. _____   "Tier" of the three-tier system that applies to wineries

4. _____   Restaurants and hotels

5. _____   Federal agency responsible for enforcing laws aimed at the illegal production of alcohol

6. _____   Federal agency that maintains the list of American Viticultural Areas

7. _____   Tier of the three-tier system that applies to wine importers

8. _____   Tier of the three-tier system that applies to wholesalers

9. _____   Federal agency responsible for enforcing laws concerning the smuggling of alcoholic beverages

10. _____   Big-box stores such as Costco and Sam's Club

11. _____   Federal agency responsible for overseeing alcohol labeling and advertising

12. _____   Wine bars

13. _____   Federal agency responsible for the collection of alcohol excise taxes

For each of the following potential elements of a wine label, determine if it is required, optional, or not permitted according to the labeling laws of the United States.

Item	Required?	Optional?	Not Permitted?
1. Vintage date _____	☐	☐	☐
2. Health claims _____	☐	☐	☐
3. Alcohol content _____	☐	☐	☐
4. Grape variety/varieties _____	☐	☐	☐
5. "Estate Bottled" _____	☐	☐	☐
6. Label art _____	☐	☐	☐
7. Name of the bottler/importer _____	☐	☐	☐
8. Address of the bottler/importer _____	☐	☐	☐
9. Net contents (volume) _____	☐	☐	☐
10. Appellation of origin _____	☐	☐	☐
11. Sulfite statement _____	☐	☐	☐
12. Brand name _____	☐	☐	☐

Mark each of the following statements as true or false.

1. _____ Some European place-names, including Chablis, Burgundy, and Chianti, are considered by the United States to be "semi-generic."

2. _____ Semi-generic place-names may be used on a US wine label as long as an American geographic term is also used, provided that the label was approved prior to March, 2006.

3. _____ The use of the term *Champagne* has never been permitted on a US wine label.

4. _____ A standard 750 ml wine bottle contains 22 fluid ounces.

5. _____ If a single vinifera grape variety appears on a California wine label, then the wine must contain a minimum of 70% of the named variety.

6. _____ Oregon Pinot Noir must contain a minimum of 90% Pinot Noir grapes.

7. _____ In the US, varietal wines produced with native North American grape varieties (*Vitis labrusca*) must contain a minimum of 75% of the named grape variety.

8. _____ The term *Meritage* refers to wines that are made with Bordeaux grape varieties.

9. _____ If a wine's stated place of origin is a country, then a minimum of 75% of the wine in the bottle must be from the named country.

10. _____ If a wine's stated place of origin is the state of California, then a minimum of 90% of the wine in the bottle must be from California.

11. _____ If a wine's appellation of origin is a specific AVA, then a minimum of 85% of the wine must be from the named AVA.

12. _____ If a wine's stated place of origin is a specific vineyard, then 100% of the wine must be from the named vineyard.

13. _____ The term *estate bottled* may not be used on American wines.

14. _____ The term *old vine* has no legal definition in the United States, but it is permitted to be used on a wine label, provided the term is not misleading.

15. _____ The term *Fumé Blanc* is an approved synonym for *Sauvignon Blanc* in the United States.

Using the map and the terms listed below, identify the following AVAs of Napa County.

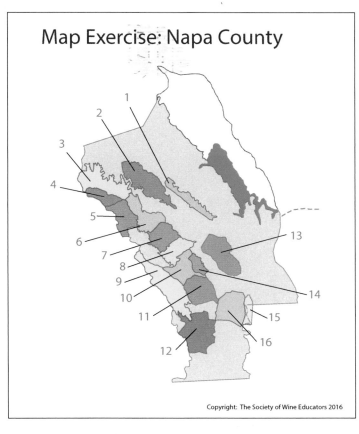

Figure 16-1: Map Exercise – Napa County

Yountville AVA
St. Helena AVA
Coombsville AVA
Oak Knoll District AVA
Wild Horse Valley AVA
Calistoga AVA
Atlas Peak AVA
Diamond Mountain
    District AVA

Spring Mountain District
    AVA
Oakville AVA
Los Carneros AVA
Chiles Valley District
    AVA
Stags Leap District AVA
Howell Mountain AVA
Rutherford AVA
Mount Veeder AVA

1. _____

2. _____

3. _____

4. _____

5. _____

6. _____

7. _____

8. _____

9. _____

10. _____

11. _____

12. _____

13. _____

14. _____

15. _____

16. _____

137

CHAPTER SIXTEEN UNITED STATES AND NORTH AMERICA

Using the map and the terms listed below, identify the following AVAs of Sonoma County.

Figure 16-2: Map Exercise – Sonoma County

Sonoma Mountain AVA
Chalk Hill AVA
Green Valley AVA
Fountaingrove District AVA
Dry Creek Valley AVA
Petaluma Gap AVA
Bennett Valley AVA
Russian River Valley AVA
Pine Mountain-Cloverdale Peak AVA
Alexander Valley AVA
Sonoma Valley AVA
Sonoma Coast AVA
Fort Ross-Seaview AVA
Moon Mountain District AVA
Rockpile AVA
Los Carneros AVA
Knights Valley AVA

1. _____
2. _____
3. _____
4. _____
5. _____
6. _____
7. _____
8. _____
9. _____
10. _____
11. _____
12. _____
13. _____
14. _____
15. _____
16. _____
17. _____

Match each of the following terms with its appropriate definition. Each term will be used only once.

Pinot Noir   Bennett Valley   Los Carneros   Fort Ross-Seaview   Wild Horse Valley
Zinfandel   Chiles Valley   Howell Mountain   Rutherford   Cole Ranch
Cabernet Sauvignon   Green Valley   Anderson Valley   Mendocino Ridge   Fountaingrove District
Petaluma Gap

1. _____ Leading red grape variety of Napa County

2. _____ Red wine grape particularly well-suited to the Russian River Valley AVA

3. _____ Mendocino County AVA well-known for sparkling wine

4. _____ Napa AVA often noted for its "dust"

5. _____ AVA shared between Napa and Sonoma Counties

6. _____ AVA shared between Napa and Solano Counties

7. _____ Subregion of the Russian River Valley AVA

8. _____ Subregion of the Sonoma Valley AVA

9. _____ AVA often referred to as "Islands in the Sky"

10. _____ AVA shared between Sonoma and Marin Counties

11. _____ Subregion of the Sonoma Coast AVA

12. _____ Leading red grape variety of the Dry Creek Valley AVA

13. _____ The smallest AVA within the United States

14. _____ The only elevation-specific AVA of Napa County

15. _____ Napa County AVA, located somewhat to the east of the valley floor, that extends into the Vaca Mountains

16. _____ AVA located (in Sonoma) just north of the Sonoma Valley AVA

Using the map and the terms listed below, identify the following AVAs of California's North Central Coast.

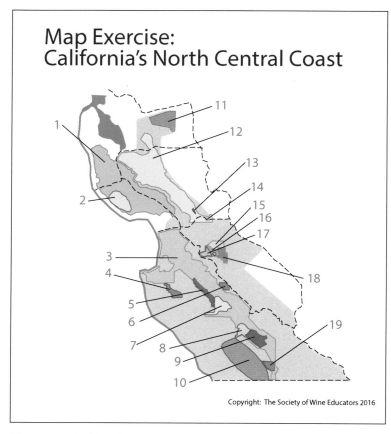

San Benito AVA
San Ysidro District AVA
San Bernabe AVA
Mount Harlan AVA
Livermore Valley AVA
Carmel Valley AVA
Chalone AVA
Hames Valley AVA
Arroyo Seco AVA
Ben Lomond Mountain AVA
San Lucas AVA
Pacheco Pass AVA
Santa Lucia Highlands AVA
Cienega Valley AVA
Paicines AVA
Santa Clara Valley AVA
Santa Cruz Mountains AVA
Monterey AVA
San Antonio Valley AVA

Figure 16-3: Map Exercise – California's North Central Coast

1. _____

2. _____

3. _____

4. _____

5. _____

6. _____

7. _____

8. _____

9. _____

10. _____

11. _____

12. _____

13. _____

14. _____

15. _____

16. _____

17. _____

18. _____

19. _____

Match each of the following terms with its appropriate definition. Each term will be used only once.

Hames Valley   Santa Maria Valley   Alta Mesa   Sierra Foothills
Livermore Valley   Edna Valley   Monterey   Central Valley
Paso Robles   Lake County   El Dorado   Ben Lomond Mountain
Guenoc Valley   Sta. Rita Hills   Arroyo Seco   Los Olivos

1. _____   AVA found within Lake County

2. _____   County that produces nearly 20% of California's Chardonnay

3. _____   Sub-appellation located in the cooler portion of the Monterey AVA

4. _____   Sub-appellation located in the warmer portion of the Monterey AVA

5. _____   Large AVA with 11 sub-appellations, including San Juan Creek and Templeton Gap

6. _____   Cool-climate AVA located in San Luis Obispo County

7. _____   AVA located mostly within the larger Santa Ynez Valley AVA

8. _____   Subregion of the Santa Cruz Mountains AVA

9. _____   Area planted with 55% of California's grape acreage

10. _____   Sub-appellation of the Lodi AVA

11. _____   Sub-appellation of the Sierra Foothills AVA

12. _____   Large AVA that contains only 1% of California's wine grape acreage

13. _____   AVA located in the far north of the Central Coast AVA

14. _____   County that, according to the EPA, has the purest air quality in California

15. _____   Santa Barbara County AVA approved in January of 2016

16. _____   The northernmost AVA in Santa Barbara County

Using the map and the terms listed below, identify the following AVAs of Washington State.

Red Mountain AVA

Columbia Gorge AVA

Walla Walla Valley AVA

Yakima Valley AVA

Wahluke Slope AVA

Snipes Mountain AVA

Lake Chelan AVA

Columbia Valley AVA

Naches Heights AVA

Rattlesnake Hills AVA

Lewis-Clark Valley AVA

Horse Heaven Hills AVA

Puget Sound AVA

Ancient Lakes of Columbia
  Valley AVA

Figure 16-4: Map Exercise – Washington State

1. _____

2. _____

3. _____

4. _____

5. _____

6. _____

7. _____

8. _____

9. _____

10. _____

11. _____

12. _____

13. _____

14. _____

Fill in the blanks or give a short answer for the following statements or questions.

1. State law requires that any wine using a Washington State appellation contain a minimum of _____ percent Washington State grapes.

2. The state of Washington is the _____ largest producer of vinifera wine in the United States.

3. The _____ of the Cascades results in near-desert conditions for much of eastern Washington State.

4. Due to the state's _____, Washington has more total sunshine hours than California.

5. The leading red grapes of Washington State are _____ and _____. While _____ is grown in smaller quantities, it often draws some of the highest critical acclaim.

6. Washington State is considered one of the premier _____ regions for Riesling.

7. The _____ AVA, one of the largest in the country, encompasses most of Washington State's vineyard area.

8. The _____ AVA was Washington State's first appellation.

9. The _____ AVA is actually a steep, southwest-facing slope near the Yakima River.

10. The _____ AVA is the only Washington State AVA located on the western side of the Cascades.

11. The _____ AVA is named for the numerous pothole lakes formed by the Missoula Floods.

12. The tiny _____ AVA , shared with Oregon, is located where the Columbia River cuts a very narrow passage through the Cascade Mountains.

13. The _____ AVA is shared between Washington State and Idaho.

Using the map and the terms listed below, identify the regional wine designations of Oregon.

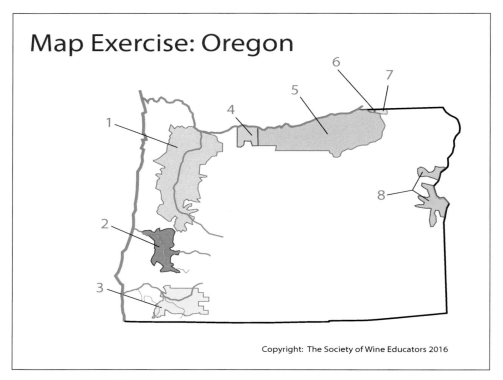

Figure 16-5: Map Exercise – Oregon

Walla Walla Valley AVA
Columbia Gorge AVA
Snake River Valley AVA
Rogue Valley AVA
Columbia Valley AVA
Umpqua Valley AVA
The Rocks of Milton-
  Freewater AVA
Willamette Valley AVA

1. _____

2. _____

3. _____

4. _____

5. _____

6. _____

7. _____

8. _____

Fill in the blanks or give a short answer for the following statements or questions.

1. What three UC Davis graduates are often credited with being the "pioneers" of the modern Oregon wine industry?

    _____

2. For what three types of wine has Oregon gained particularly wide acclaim?

    _____

3. What top Burgundy producer established a wine estate in Oregon in 1988, and what is the name of the winery?

    _____

    _____

4. What three AVAs straddle the Oregon-Washington State border?

    _____

    _____

5. The _____ AVA, located just south of Portland, is divided into the following seven sub-appellations:

    _____

    _____

    _____

    _____

6. The tiny _____ AVA is located in the Oregon side of the larger Walla Walla Valley AVA, which is itself shared with _____
    _____ .

7. The _____ AVA is a subregion of the Rogue Valley AVA located in the far south of Oregon.

8. While the Willamette Valley is relatively cool, the vineyards in the southwest of Oregon, located in the valleys of the _____ and _____ Rivers, are warmer, and better suited to grapes such as Merlot and Cabernet Sauvignon.

Using the map and the terms listed below, identify the AVAs of the Willamette Valley.

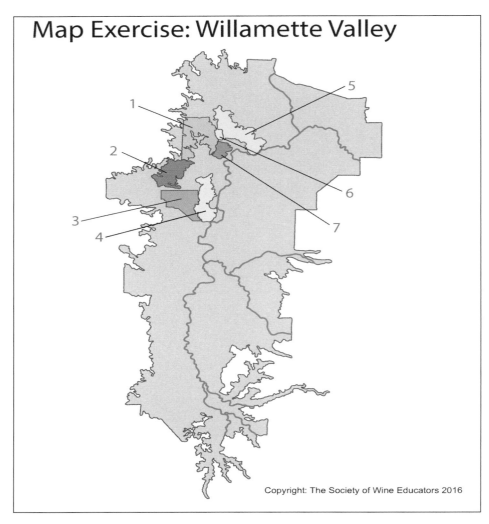

Eola-Amity Hills AVA
Ribbon Ridge AVA
McMinnville AVA
Dundee Hills AVA
Chehalem Mountains AVA
Yamhill-Carlton AVA
Van Duzer Corridor AVA

1. _____

2. _____

3. _____

4. _____

5. _____

6. _____

7. _____

Figure 16-6: Map Exercise – Willamette Valley

Fill in the blanks or give a short answer for the following statements or questions.

1. New York's _____ AVA and its two sub-AVAs, the _____
    AVA and the _____ AVA, account for over 85% of the state's wine production.

2. A viticulturist from Russia named _____ is credited with
    championing the planting of vinifera grapes in the cold-climate environment of New York State.

3. With a climate similar to Germany's, New York State does well with grapes from the _____
    _____ species and cold-hardy _____, in addition to vinifera
    varieties such as Riesling and Cabernet Franc.

4. The _____ AVA is located two hours east of New York City. It has two sub-
    appellations, including the North Fork of Long Island AVA and the _____ AVA.

5. The Brotherhood Winery is located in the _____ AVA, located north of
    New York City.

6. The wine laws of Ontario are defined by an appellation and quality-control system known as the

    _____ .

7. The majority of Canada's wine grapes are grown on the shores of the Great Lakes in the province of

    _____ .

8. The _____ appellation is home to most of the
    vineyards in Ontario.

9. A ridge of cliffs known as the _____ has a major
    effect on the climate of the Niagara Peninsula region, giving the area a wide range of microclimates.

10. The premier grape growing area in British Columbia, found east of the Coast Range, is the

    _____ .

11. The main wine region in Baja California is the _____,
    located near the city of _____ .

12. _____, located in the Mexican state of Coahuila, is one of the oldest
    wineries in North America.

1. Which of the following properly states the three tiers in the three-tier distribution system of the United States?
   a. Producers, importers, and wholesalers
   b. Producers, distributors, and retailers
   c. Suppliers, retailers, and on-premise
   d. Wholesalers, distributors, and importers

2. Which of the following elements are *all* required on a US wine label?
   a. Alcohol content, address of the bottler, and vintage date
   b. Brand name, net contents by volume, and appellation of origin
   c. Name of the bottler, grape varieties, and brand name
   d. Brand name, alcohol content, and net contents by volume

3. Which of the following wines could be labeled with the term *Meritage*?
   a. A red blend of Cabernet Sauvignon, Cabernet Franc, and Merlot
   b. A red blend of Petit Verdot, Malbec, and Pinot Noir
   c. A white blend of Sauvignon Blanc and Chenin Blanc
   d. A white blend of Chardonnay and Semillon

4. If a wine's appellation of origin is Napa Valley, what percentage of its contents must be from the Napa Valley AVA?
   a. 100%
   b. Minimum of 95%
   c. Minimum of 85%
   d. Minimum of 75%

5. If a wine is labeled as "Napa Valley Sauvignon Blanc," what percentage of the wine must be Sauvignon Blanc?
   a. 100%
   b. Minimum of 95%
   c. Minimum of 85%
   d. Minimum of 75%

6. What is the leading red grape of Napa County?
   a. Merlot
   b. Cabernet Sauvignon
   c. Pinot Noir
   d. Zinfandel

7. Which of the following AVAs is the smallest in the United States?
   a. Guenoc Valley
   b. Rockpile
   c. Howell Mountain
   d. Cole Ranch

8. Which of the following AVAs is a subregion of the Russian River Valley AVA?
   a. Fort Ross-Seaview
   b. Green Valley
   c. Chiles Valley
   d. Los Carneros

9. Of the following AVAs, which is best known for Zinfandel?
   a. Dry Creek Valley
   b. McMinnville
   c. Anderson Valley
   d. Dundee Hills

10. Of the following AVAs, which is best known for Pinot Noir?
    a. Knights Valley
    b. Borden Ranch
    c. Eola-Amity Hills
    d. Paso Robles

11. Which of the following is a Mendocino County AVA well-known for sparkling wine?
    a. Rockpile
    b. Anderson Valley
    c. Ribbon Ridge
    d. Red Mountain

12. Which of the following is a Washington State AVA well-known for Cabernet Sauvignon?
    a. McMinnville
    b. Arroyo Grande
    c. Edna Valley
    d. Snipes Mountain

13. Which of the following AVAs covers a large expanse of land, yet contains only 1% of California's vineyard acreage?
    a. Livermore Valley
    b. Central Valley
    c. Lodi
    d. Sierra Foothills

14. The Paso Robles AVA is located within which of the following counties?
    a. El Dorado
    b. Monterey
    c. San Luis Obispo
    d. Santa Barbara

15. Which of the following are *all* subregions of the Lodi AVA?
    a. Jahant, Borden Ranch, and Alta Mesa
    b. Alta Mesa, Hames Valley, and Borden Ranch
    c. Edna Valley, Clements Hills, and Sloughhouse
    d. Borden Ranch, Snipes Mountain, and Ribbon Ridge

16. Which of the following mountain ranges provides a rain shadow for much of eastern Washington State?
    a. The Coastal Range
    b. The Cascades
    c. The Caribou Mountains
    d. The Snake River Range

17. David Lett and Dick Erath are considered two of the "pioneers" of the wine industry in which of the following areas?
    a. Napa Valley
    b. Finger Lakes
    c. Mendocino
    d. Oregon

18. Which of the following wine regions is most affected by the Niagara Escarpment?
    a. Okanagan Valley
    b. Ontario
    c. Hudson River Region
    d. Clear Lake

19. Due to the region's climate, which of the following grapes are considered to be best suited for the Finger Lakes AVA?
    a. Zinfandel and Sauvignon Blanc
    b. Syrah and Riesling
    c. Cabernet Franc and Riesling
    d. Chardonnay and Malbec

20. During what years was Prohibition in effect in the United States?
    a. 1917–1925
    b. 1920–1933
    c. 1915–1929
    d. 1925–1933

SOUTH AMERICA

CHAPTER SEVENTEEN

LEARNING OBJECTIVES

After studying this chapter, the candidate should be able to:
- Recognize the importance of latitude and elevation for grape growing in South America.
- Describe the influences of the Andes on grape growing in Argentina and Chile.

- Discuss the major wine regions of Argentina and Chile.
- Recall the significant grape varieties grown in Argentina and Chile.
- Understand the general status of the wine industry in Brazil and Uruguay.

EXERCISE 1: ARGENTINA: SHORT ANSWER/FILL IN THE BLANK

Fill in the blanks or give a short answer for the following statements or questions.

1. What climatic and geographical features combine to make the western foothills of Argentina an excellent area for wine grapes?

   _____

2. What is the name of the fierce winter wind that often affects the vineyards of Argentina?

   _____

3. What weather threat can affect the vineyards of Argentina at harvest time?

   _____

4. What is the leading red grape of Argentina?_____

5. What is considered the "signature" white grape of Argentina?_____

6. What is the highest level of wine quality designation used in Argentina?

   _____

7. What is the intermediate quality level designation used for the wines of Argentina?

   _____

8. What designation is used for table wines and regional wines in Argentina?

   _____

9. What are the first two regions in Argentina to be declared DOC?

   _____

Using the map and the terms listed below, identify the following wine regions of Argentina.

Chubut
Córdoba
Buenos Aires
Tucamán
Mendoza
Salta
Río Negro
Catamarca
San Juan
La Rioja
Jujuy
Neuquén
La Pampa

1. _____

2. _____

3. _____

4. _____

5. _____

6. _____

7. _____

8. _____

9. _____

10. _____

11. _____

12. _____

13. _____

Figure 17-1: Map Exercise – Argentina

Match each of the following terms with its appropriate definition. Each term will be used only once.

Salta	Reserva	Neuquén	Chubut
Pedro Giménez	San Juan	La Rioja	Jujuy
Río Negro	Cafayate	Bonarda	San Rafael
Vinos finos	Mendoza	Luján de Cuyo	Córdoba

1. _____ Province with close to 17% of Argentina's vineyards, making it the second-largest grape-producing province in the country

2. _____ Province particularly well-known for high-altitude Torrontés Riojano

3. _____ Province that contains the Famatina mountain range

4. _____ Province that contains close to 75% of Argentina's vineyards

5. _____ Term used to designate the best wines of Argentina

6. _____ Home province of the ultra-high-elevation Moya Vineyard

7. _____ Label term based on minimum aging periods

8. _____ DOC region located in Mendoza's Primera Zona

9. _____ Province that contains some of the lowest elevation vineyards in Argentina

10. _____ A subregion of Salta with very high-altitude vineyards

11. _____ Province located in the geographic center of Argentina (to the east of La Rioja)

12. _____ Province located just south of Mendoza

13. _____ Red grape also known as Douce Noir

14. _____ White grape grown primarily for use in fortified wines and bulk wines

15. _____ DOC region located in South Mendoza

16. _____ Home province of the Sarmiento region (and some of the southernmost vineyards in the world)

Fill in the blanks or give a short answer for the following statements or questions.

1. Chile is a long, narrow country, almost _____ miles in length, and rarely more than _____ miles wide.

2. The _____, one of the driest places on earth, is located in the north of Chile, while the south contains the frozen archipelago of

   _____ .

3. In part due to its natural barriers and strict quarantine policies, Chile has managed to remain free of the vineyard pest _____ .

4. Chile has a cold ocean current, known as the _____ Current, flowing along its shores from the polar seas.

5. _____ is the most widely planted grape in Chile.

6. In the 1990s, it was discovered that many of the Chilean grapes thought to be Merlot were actually _____, which is now considered by many to be the "signature" grape of Chile.

7. Some of the Chilean grapes originally thought to be Sauvignon Blanc are actually _____, and many of these vines have been replaced. However, the two grapes are not always differentiated, and both of the grapes (and their wines) are sometimes simply referred to as _____ .

8. Chile has a set of geographic place-of-origin laws known as the _____ system.

9. Under Chilean law, the minimum requirement for place of origin, vintage, and variety on a wine label is _____ percent; however, many export-oriented wineries use the EU standard of _____ .

10. As of 2011, three terms based on Chile's east–west geography were approved for use on Chilean wine labels. What are they?

    _____

    _____

    _____

Using the map and the terms listed below, identify the following wine regions of Chile.

Map Exercise: Chile

Copyright: The Society of Wine Educators 2016

Figure 17-2: Map Exercise – Chile

Curicó Valley
Rapel Valley
San Antonio Valley
Itata Valley
Limarí Valley
Maipo Valley
Malleco Valley
Elqui Valley
Maule Valley
Aconcagua Valley
Bío-Bío Valley
Choapa Valley
Casablanca Valley

1. _____

2. _____

3. _____

4. _____

5. _____

6. _____

7. _____

8. _____

9. _____

10. _____

11. _____

12. _____

13. _____

Match each of the following terms with its appropriate definition. Each term will be used only once.

Bío-Bío Valley	Casablanca Valley	Leyda Valley	Austral Region
Rapel Valley	Curicó Valley	Central Valley	Elqui Valley
Choapa Valley	Maule Valley	Limarí Valley	
Atacama Region	Maipo Valley	Aconcagua Valley	

1. _____ Region surrounding the Chilean city of Santiago

2. _____ A cool-climate subregion of the Coquimbo, well-known for mineral-driven white wines

3. _____ The region that contains the Cachapoal and Colchagua Valleys

4. _____ The warmest subregion of Aconcagua

5. _____ A region of the Central Valley located inland, with no maritime influence

6. _____ A large area that encompasses more than 80% of Chile's vineyards

7. _____ Northern region better known for Pisco than for fine wine

8. _____ Region located where the valley floor widens at the southern end of the Central Valley

9. _____ The southernmost extreme of winegrowing in Chile

10. _____ Region with the highest rainfall of all of Chile's wine regions

11. _____ Subregion of the Aconcagua located very close to the coast and well-known for white wines

12. _____ A subzone of the San Antonio Valley known for granite soils and breezy conditions

13. _____ Area located very close to the edge of the Atacama Desert

14. _____ Wine area located at the narrowest point of the country

1. What is considered to be the "signature" white grape of Argentina?
   a. Chardonnay
   b. Pedro Giménez
   c. Torrontés
   d. Sauvignon Blanc

2. What is the Zonda?
   a. A cold ocean current that runs up the coast of Argentina
   b. A cold ocean current that runs up the coast of Chile
   c. A hot, dry breeze that affects the Central Valley of Chile
   d. A fierce wind that may affect the vineyards of Argentina

3. What is the Humboldt Current?
   a. A cold ocean current that runs up the coast of Argentina
   b. A cold ocean current that runs up the coast of Chile
   c. A warm ocean current that runs down the coast of Chile
   d. A warm summer current that affects all of the Southern Hemisphere

4. What adverse weather condition often affects the vineyards of Argentina at harvest time?
   a. Sudden freezes
   b. Extreme humidity that can cause fungal problems
   c. Hurricanes
   d. Hailstorms

5. Which of the following grapes, once widely grown in Bordeaux, has become a "signature" grape of Chile?
   a. Malbec
   b. Petite Verdot
   c. Carmenère
   d. Semillon

6. Which of the following wine regions is located nearest to the border between Argentina and Bolivia?
   a. Jujuy
   b. Mendoza
   c. La Rioja
   d. Catamarca

7. Which of the following wine regions is known for high-altitude Torrontés?
   a. Cafayate
   b. Maule Valley
   c. Malleco Valley
   d. Río Negro

8. What is the most widely planted grape in Chile?
   a. Pinot Noir
   b. Merlot
   c. Cabernet Sauvignon
   d. Carmenère

9. Which of the following grape varieties is often mistaken for Sauvignon Blanc in Chile?
   a. Sauvignon Gris
   b. Sauvignon Vert
   c. Chenin Blanc
   d. Viognier

10. Which of the following wine regions is located closest to the city of Santiago?
    a. Mendoza
    b. Coquimbo
    c. Maipo Valley
    d. Maipú Valley

11. Which of the following areas has been awarded Brazil's first DO designation?
    a. Serra Gaúcha
    b. Serra do Sudeste
    c. Planalto Catarinense
    d. Vale dos Vinhedos

AUSTRALIA AND NEW ZEALAND

CHAPTER EIGHTEEN

LEARNING OBJECTIVES

After studying this chapter, the candidate should be able to:

- Discuss the general roles and positions of Australia and New Zealand in the global wine industry.
- Describe the basic elements of the Australian appellation system and wine labeling laws.
- Identify the physical locations and general climates of Australia's and New Zealand's major wine regions.
- Recall the significant grape varieties grown in Australia and New Zealand.

EXERCISE 1: AUSTRALIAN WINE: FILL IN THE BLANK/SHORT ANSWER

Fill in the blanks or give a short answer for the following statements or questions.

1. What is the most widely planted grape in Australia?_____

2. What three grape varieties are used in the production of Australian Rhône-style blends, known as "GSM"?

   _____

3. What is the name of Australia's place-of-origin system for wine?

   _____

4. Put the following terms used for Australian wine regions in the proper order, from largest to smallest in terms of geographic size: zone, region, state.

   _____

5. If an Australian wine uses a varietal name, what percentage of the wine must be made using the named grape variety?_____

6. Australia is the first country to require a_____ date on some styles of wine, but it is usually only seen on_____ products.

7. What nickname is often used for Australian sweet wines?_____

8. What agency is in charge of enforcing the place-of-origin system of wine in Australia?

   _____

Using the map and the terms listed below, identify the following wine regions of Australia.

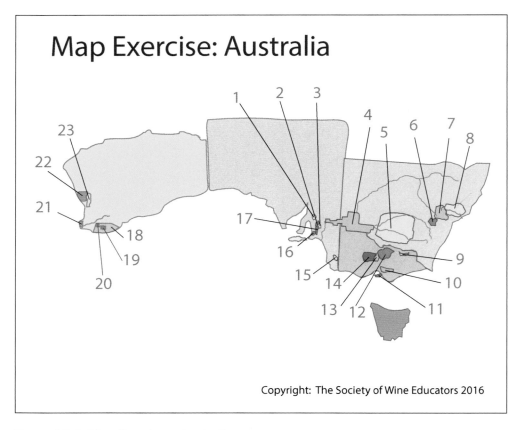

Figure 18-1: Map Exercise – Australia

Adelaide Hills	Clare Valley	1. _____	13. _____
Heathcote	Goulburn Valley	2. _____	14. _____
Barossa Valley	Perth Hills	3. _____	15. _____
Frankland	Riverina	4. _____	16. _____
Mudgee	McLaren Vale	5. _____	17. _____
Murray Darling	Bendigo	6. _____	18. _____
Margaret River	Mount Barker	7. _____	19. _____
Hunter	Orange	8. _____	20. _____
Rutherglen	Yarra Valley	9. _____	21. _____
Mornington Peninsula	Eden Valley	10. _____	22. _____
Swan District	Great Southern	11. _____	23. _____
Coonawarra		12. _____	

EXERCISE 3: AUSTRALIA: MATCHING

Match each of the following terms with its appropriate definition. Each term will be used only once.

Coonawarra   Tasmania   Heathcote   Riverland
Barossa Valley   Yarra Valley   South Eastern Australia   Margaret River
Riverina   Mudgee   Limestone Coast
Clare Valley   Hunter Valley   Rutherglen

1. _____   The largest wine region in Australia, according to geographic area

2. _____   Zone that includes Coonawarra

3. _____   A multistate GI

4. _____   Warm climate zone north of Sydney noted for Semillon

5. _____   Region well-known for Terra Rosa

6. _____   Region in Victoria known for fortified Muscat wines

7. _____   Island located off the coast of Victoria; known for cool-climate wines

8. _____   Region near Adelaide known for Shiraz

9. _____   Region located in Southwest Australia

10. _____   Region located on the west side of the Great Dividing Range; contains vineyards approaching 2,000 feet in elevation

11. _____   Commercially important region with the second largest volume of wine production in Australia

12. _____   Region near Adelaide known for Riesling

13. _____   Region on the outskirts of Melbourne noted for Pinot Noir and Chardonnay

14. _____   Region located between Bendigo and Goulburn Valley that is influenced by the cool winds from the Mt. Camel Range

Fill in the blanks or give a short answer for the following statements or questions.

1. When did New Zealand begin to establish its modern wine industry? _____

    _____

2. Where is New Zealand located? _____

    _____

3. What mountain chain runs the length of New Zealand's South Island?

    _____

4. What effect does this mountain range have on the climate of New Zealand?

    _____

    _____

5. What factors account for New Zealand's cool climate? _____

    _____

6. Due to the country's unique climate, where are most of the vineyards in New Zealand located?

    _____

    _____

7. What percentage of New Zealand's wine production is white wine? _____

8. What is the most widely planted white grape of New Zealand? _____

9. What are the other leading white wine grapes of New Zealand? _____

    _____

10. What is the most widely planted red grape of New Zealand?

    _____

11. What are the other leading red grapes of New Zealand? _____

    _____

Using the map and the terms listed below, identify the following wine regions of New Zealand.

Figure 18-2: Map Exercise – New Zealand

Hawke's Bay
Marlborough
Nelson
Waikato/Bay of Plenty
Auckland
Wairarapa
Canterbury
Northland
Otago/Central Otago
Gisborne
Waitaki Valley

1. _____

2. _____

3. _____

4. _____

5. _____

6. _____

7. _____

8. _____

9. _____

10. _____

11. _____

Match each of the following terms with its appropriate definition. Each term will be used only once.

Gimblett Gravels   Canterbury   Aotearoa   Banks Peninsula   Waikato
Marlborough   Nelson   Awatere Valley   Hawke's Bay   Waitaki Valley
Gisborne   Central Otago   Waipara Valley   Wairau Valley   Poverty Bay

1. _____ Area located within the Gisborne region

2. _____ The self-proclaimed "Chardonnay capital of New Zealand"

3. _____ Nickname meaning "Land of the Long White Cloud"

4. _____ Region where Cloudy Bay Vineyards is located

5. _____ Region known for stony, alluvial soils and a cool climate that tends to become drier as one heads inland

6. _____ Large landmass jutting eastward from the city of Christchurch

7. _____ Area within the Hawke's Bay region known for greywacke soils

8. _____ The only wine region on New Zealand's South Island located west of the Southern Alps

9. _____ Subregion of Marlborough located to the south of the Wairau Valley

10. _____ Another name used for the Bay of Plenty

11. _____ Large wine region that contains the city of Christchurch

12. _____ Subregion of North Canterbury

13. _____ Leading region for New Zealand Cabernet Sauvignon, Merlot, and Syrah

14. _____ Wine region located along the border of Canterbury and Otago

15. _____ The southernmost wine region on New Zealand's South Island

1. What three grapes typically make up the Australian GSM blend?
   a. Grenache, Shiraz, and Merlot
   b. Graciano, Shiraz, and Malbec
   c. Grenache, Shiraz, and Mourvèdre
   d. Grenache, Shiraz, and Malbec

2. Which of the following has the most impact on the climate of New Zealand?
   a. The Humboldt Current
   b. The Southern Alps
   c. The Great Dividing Range
   d. The Zonda Winds

3. Which of the following properly states the categories used in Australia's Geographical Indications, from largest in size to smallest?
   a. State, Region, Zone
   b. Region, Zone, State
   c. Zone, Region, State
   d. State, Zone, Region

4. Which of the following wine regions is located farthest south?
   a. Tasmania
   b. Canterbury
   c. Nelson
   d. Central Otago

5. If an Australian wine uses a varietal name, what percentage of the wine must be made from the named grape variety?
   a. A minimum of 75%
   b. A minimum of 80%
   c. A minimum of 85%
   d. A minimum of 95%

6. Which of the following New Zealand wine areas grows the most Cabernet Sauvignon?
   a. Hawke's Bay
   b. Central Otago
   c. Nelson
   d. Marlborough

7. Which of the following Australian regions are both well-known for Riesling?
   a. Clare Valley and Eden Valley
   b. Margaret River and Edna Valley
   c. Hunter Valley and Clare Valley
   d. Eden Valley and McDowell Valley

8. Which of the following New Zealand wine regions is located west of the Southern Alps?
   a. Heathcote
   b. Nelson
   c. Awatere Valley
   d. Hawke's Bay

9. Which of the following Australian regions is noted for Semillon?
   a. Hunter Valley
   b. Rutherglen
   c. Tasmania
   d. Riverland

10. What is the most widely planted red grape variety in New Zealand?
    a. Merlot
    b. Gamay
    c. Pinot Noir
    d. Cabernet Sauvignon

11. The Muscat of Alexandria grape is grown in many of the warmer areas of Australia, where it is often called:
    a. Criolla
    b. Bonamico
    c. Counoise
    d. Gordo Blanco

12. What is the most widely planted white grape in Australia?
    a. Sauvignon Blanc
    b. Chardonnay
    c. Chenin Blanc
    d. Semillon

UNIT THREE WINE LABELS, LAWS, AND REGIONS

LEARNING OBJECTIVES

After studying this chapter, the candidate should be able to:

- Discuss the physical location and general climate of South Africa's major wine regions.
- Describe the significant grape varieties grown in South Africa.

- Recall South African synonyms for international grape varieties.
- Describe the basic elements of the South African appellation system and wine labeling laws.

EXERCISE 1: AFRICA: FILL IN THE BLANK/SHORT ANSWER

Fill in the blanks or give a short answer for the following statements or questions.

1. What year were vines first planted in South Africa?_____

2. How does the Benguela Current influence the climate of the vineyards of South Africa?

   _____

3. What is the most widely planted grape in South Africa, and by what local name is it known?

   _____

4. What is a "Noble Late Harvest" wine? _____

5. What is a Cape Blend? _____

   _____

6. What is the name of the appellation system used in South Africa? _____

7. Put the following terms used for South African wine regions in the proper order, from largest to smallest (according to geographic size): district, geographical unit, ward, region. _____

   _____

Using the map and the terms listed below, identify the following wine regions of South Africa.

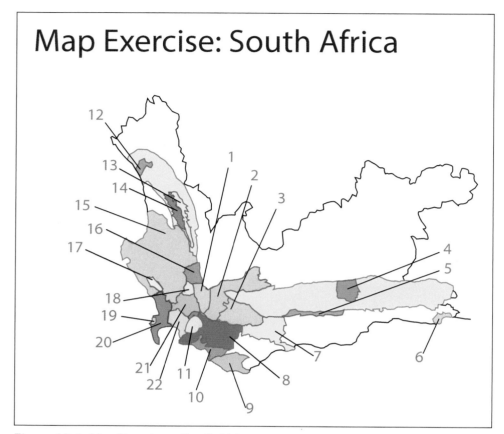

Figure 19-1: Map Exercise – South Africa

1. _____

2. _____

3. _____

4. _____

5. _____

6. _____

7. _____

8. _____

9. _____

10. _____

11. _____

12. _____

13. _____

14. _____

15. _____

16. _____

17. _____

18. _____

19. _____

20. _____

21. _____

22. _____

Cape Agulhas

Robertson

Constantia

Wellington

Stellenbosch

Citrusdal Valley

Elgin

Calitzdorp

Darling

Plettenberg Bay

Walker Bay

Lutzville Valley

Breedekloof

Citrusdal Mountain

Tulbagh

Worcester

Langeberg-Garcia

Overberg

Swartland

Swellendam

Paarl

Cape Town

EXERCISE 3: AFRICA: MATCHING

Match each of the following terms with its appropriate definition. Each term will be used only once.

Devon Valley   Cape Town   Stellenbosch   Robertson   Swartland
Drakenstein Valley Paarl   Worcester   Constantia   Algeria
Northern Cape   Franschhoek Valley Walker Bay   Western Cape

1. _____ Cool-climate district near the town of Hermanus; known for Chardonnay and Pinot Noir

2. _____ District known as "the Valley of Wine and Roses"

3. _____ Former French colony that once produced over 200 million cases of wine a year

4. _____ Rugged area where dry farming and untrellised vines are used

5. _____ District that contains seven wards, including Devon Valley and Bottelary

6. _____ One of the seven wards of the Stellenbosch District

7. _____ Inland district that grows 25% of South Africa's wine (as well as table grapes and grapes for brandy)

8. _____ District in the Coastal Region whose name means "French Corner"

9. _____ Geographical Unit located well inland that contains less than 5% of the country's vines

10. _____ Ward near the city of Cape Town that is famous for a traditional desert wine

11. _____ District north of Stellenbosch that is home to many of the more familiar South African wine brands

12. _____ This Geographical Unit contains nearly 95% of South Africa's vineyards

13. _____ Area settled by French Huguenots in the 1700s

14. _____ District that contains the Constantia Ward and the Hout Bay Ward

1. In the context of South Africa's "Wine of Origin" scheme, which of the following terms represents the smallest possible geographic area?
   a. Geographical Unit
   b. Ward
   c. Region
   d. District

2. Which of the following two grapes were crossed to create the Pinotage grape variety?
   a. Pinot Noir and Merlot
   b. Cabernet Sauvignon and Pinot Noir
   c. Cinsault and Pinot Noir
   d. Shiraz and Cabernet Sauvignon

3. Which of the following climatic conditions is due to the influence of the Benguela Current?
   a. The rain shadow of the Drakenstein Mountains
   b. The "Roaring 40s" winds
   c. The Santa Ana winds
   d. The Cape Doctor

4. What is Steen?
   a. An alternative name for the Muscat of Alexandria grape variety
   b. A hybrid grape made by a Riesling X Muscat cross
   c. A botrytis-affected dessert wine
   d. An alternative name for the Chenin Blanc grape variety

5. Which of the following is a cool-climate South African wine district, well-known for Pinot Noir?
   a. Walker Bay
   b. Robertson
   c. Stellenbosch
   d. Paarl

6. Which of the following wards has a long history of producing a well-known dessert wine?
   a. Stellenbosch
   b. Breede River Valley
   c. Swartland
   d. Constantia

7. Winemaking in Franschhoek Valley was highly influenced by which group of people?
   a. Dutch traders
   b. English immigrants
   c. American settlers
   d. French Huguenots

8. The majority of South Africa's vineyard area is located within which of the following Geographical Units?
   a. The Northern Cape
   b. Breede River Valley
   c. The Western Cape
   d. Boberg

9. Which area is located farthest south?
   a. Lutzville Valley
   b. Cape Agulhas
   c. Wellington
   d. Swartland

10. The Boberg regional designation is used to refer to which of the following?
    a. Fortified wines
    b. Sparkling wines
    c. Cape Blends
    d. Wines produced from 100-year-old vines

ASIA

LEARNING OBJECTIVES

After studying this chapter, the candidate should be able to:

- Describe the recent growth of the culture and business of wine in China.
- Discuss the physical location and general attributes of the wine-producing regions of China.

- Recall the main grape varieties used in Chinese wine.
- Describe the grape-based wine industry in Japan.
- Discuss the wines produced in south, Southeast, and Equatorial Asia.

EXERCISE 1: WINES OF CHINA: FILL IN THE BLANK

Fill in the blanks or give a short answer for the following statements or questions.

1. The modern era of Chinese wine production is considered to have begun in the year _____, when a _____ Dynasty diplomat imported over 100 European grape varieties into China.

2. The first modern Chinese winery, now known as the Changyu Pioneer Wine Company, Inc. is located in the _____ province.

3. By geographic area, China is the _____ largest country in the world.

4. Of the many crosses and hybrid grapes created in grape-breeding programs, _____, a Muscat Hamburg X Alicante Bouschet cross used for its deep red color, is one of the most successful.

5. The _____ grape, a Muscat Hamburg X *Vitis amurensis* hybrid, is widely used for its extreme cold resistance.

6. _____ is the name used in some parts of China to refer to the Carmenère grape variety.

7. _____, a French Cabernet Sauvignon X Grenache cross, is among the most successful red grapes in China.

8. Longyan is an aromatic grape that often goes by the name of _____.

9. Approved in 2012, _____ is the first legally regulated and geographically defined wine region in China.

Using the map and the terms listed below, identify the wine growing regions of China.

Beijing	Shanxi	Yunnan	Hebei	Xinjiang
Tianjin	Gansu	Ningxia	Shandong	Shaanxi

1. _____

2. _____

3. _____

4. _____

5. _____

6. _____

7. _____

8. _____

9. _____

10. _____

Figure 20-1: Map Exercise – China

Match each of the following terms with its appropriate definition. Terms may be used more than once.

Yunnan   Hebei   Ningxia   Shandong   Hebei   Shanxi   Xinjiang

1. _____   Home to the Sino-French Demonstration Vineyard

2. _____   Region located in the extreme west of China, neighboring the country of Kazakhstan

3. _____   Area where a French missionary first planted a French grape known as Rose Honey

4. _____   Region that has established a five-level classification for wineries

5. _____   Wine region located in the area surrounding the municipality of Beijing

6. _____   The southernmost wine region in China

7. _____   The Heshuo/Hoxud wine region, which obtained Geographical Indication status in 2015, is located here

8. _____   Region located on the ocean, mostly south of the Yellow River

9. _____   The home of Grace Vineyards

10. _____   This area is home to the China Great Wall Wine Company

11. _____   Area that includes the Eastern Foot of Helan Mountain wine region

12. _____   Home to the Shangri-La Winery Company Limited

13. _____   Region located on the eastern edge of the Gobi Desert

14. _____   The wines of this area were described by the famous explorer Marco Polo

Mark each of the following statements as true or false.

1. _____ Portuguese wine was first imported into Japan in the sixteenth century.

2. _____ Japanese per capita wine consumption is among the lowest in Asia.

3. _____ Japan has traditionally been more closely associated with the production and consumption of rice wine (sake) than grape-based wine.

4. _____ Four islands—Hokkaido, Honshu, Shikoku, and Kyushu—are home to a large percentage of the Japanese population.

5. _____ The Koshu grape variety, a descendant of European grapes, is considered to be native to Japan.

6. _____ Koshu is a red grape variety used mainly to produce low-tannin, fruity, semi-sweet red wines.

7. _____ According to legend, a Buddhist monk planted the first vineyards in Japan after a vision of the Yakushi Buddha.

8. _____ Muscat Bailey-A is a red hybrid grape created at the Iwanohara Winery.

9. _____ Hokkaido is considered the "main island" of Japan.

10. _____ The first modern Japanese wine was produced in 1874 at Kōfu.

11. _____ In 1990, the Koshu grape variety was officially recognized as a wine grape by the International Organization of Vine and Wine.

12. _____ Japan passed its first meaningful wine regulations in 2005.

13. _____ The Yamanashi Prefecture and the island of Hokkaido have both been awarded geographical indications for wine.

14. _____ The sakoku policy encouraged internationalism and allowed many freedoms in terms of commerce and trade.

15. _____ Muscat Bailey-A is sometimes used in red wine blends along with vinifera grape varieties.

1. Which of the following was considered to be modern China's first winery?
   a. Grace Vineyards
   b. Sula Winery
   c. Takla Makan Winery
   d. Changyu Winemaking Company

2. In terms of geographic area, China is considered to be the _____ largest country in the world.
   a. First
   b. Second
   c. Third
   d. Fourth

3. Which of the following areas is located farthest west?
   a. Hebei
   b. Ningxia
   c. Xinjiang
   d. Yunnan

4. Which of the following are the parent grapes of Yan 73?
   a. Muscat Hamburg and Alicante Bouschet
   b. Red Globe and Chenin Blanc
   c. Rose Honey and Chardonnay
   d. Cabernet Sauvignon and Merlot

5. Which of the following grape varieties is a Cabernet Sauvignon X Grenache cross?
   a. Cabernet Gernischt
   b. Marselan
   c. Herbemont
   d. Marufo

6. Which of the following names can be translated as "north of the river"?
   a. Hebei
   b. Shanxi
   c. Yunnan
   d. Dalat

7. Which of the following best describes the location of Ningxia?
   a. On the shores of the Yellow Sea, between Shanghai and Beijing
   b. An island in the Pacific Ocean, to the west of Hong Kong
   c. About 500 miles west of Beijing
   d. In the extreme west of China, on the border with Afghanistan

8. Which of the following is a Chinese wine area located mostly south of the Yangtze River?
   a. Shanxi
   b. Yunnan
   c. Shandong
   d. Kyushu

9. Which of the following best describes the Koshu grape variety?
   a. A pink-skinned grape that is quite successful in Japan
   b. A red hybrid that is used for its intense red color
   c. A red vinifera variety that is grown in Bali
   d. A white labrusca variety that is successful in India's Tamil Nadu region

10. Which of the following is a red hybrid grape, considered to be native to Japan?
    a. Rose Honey
    b. Red Misket
    c. Muscat Bailey-A
    d. Melnik

WINE
CONSUMPTION
AND SERVICE

UNIT FOUR

THE SENSORY EVALUATION OF WINE

CHAPTER TWENTY-ONE

LEARNING OBJECTIVES

After studying this chapter, the candidate should be able to:

- Describe the physiological processes of sight, smell, and taste.
- Identify visual clues concerning a wine's characteristics.
- Recognize the differences between detection threshold and recognition threshold.
- Discuss the differences between aromas, flavors, and taste sensations.
- Recall general procedures for setting up a wine tasting.
- Understand the techniques used in evaluating wine.

EXERCISE 1: UNDERSTANDING THE SENSES: MATCHING

Match each of the following terms with its appropriate definition. Each term will be used only once.

Sweet	Volatile components	Bitter	Umami
Recognition threshold	Perception	Detection threshold	Sensation
Flavor	Olfactory epithelium	Stimulus	

1. _____ A chemical, physical, or thermal activator that can produce a sensory response

2. _____ Molecules that are able to become airborne

3. _____ The neurological response to a stimulus in the environment

4. _____ The brain's interpretation of any information gathered by the senses

5. _____ The smallest amount of a stimulus necessary to trigger an unidentifiable sensation

6. _____ The smallest amount of a stimulus necessary to trigger an identifiable sensation

7. _____ Sensory organ for the sense of smell

8. _____ Term used for the combination of tastes, aromas, and other sensations experienced in wine

9. _____ Humans are most sensitive to this taste component

10. _____ Humans are least sensitive to this taste component

11. _____ The taste of glutamic acid, sometimes referred to as "the protein taste"

Fill in the blanks with an appropriate color descriptor for each style of wine.

WHITE WINE COLORS:

_____ Found in young white table wines from cool growing regions

_____ Found in white wines made from grapes that have not reached optimal ripeness or maturity

_____ The standard hue for most young dry white wines

_____ Found in older white wines

_____ Found in young white wines from warm growing regions

_____ Found in white wines that have spent some time in barrels

_____ May be indicative of a maderized or oxidized white wine

RED WINE COLORS:

_____ Found in young reds

_____ Found in older, mature reds

_____ Found in high-acid reds

_____ Found in low-acid reds

_____ May be indicative of an oxidized red wine

Fill in the blanks for the following statements or questions.

1. The average recognition threshold for sugar in wine is around _____ percent.

2. Very few people will notice the sweetness of a wine with a residual sugar level of _____ or below.

3. The perception of sweetness in a wine can be masked by the presence of _____ or _____.

4. Wine tasters refer to the thickness or viscosity of wine as _____.

5. Young red wines with high levels of tannin can be described as _____.

6. A wine with a high level of alcohol may produce a _____ tactile sensation as well as a _____ taste for some people; hypersensitive tasters may perceive alcohol as a _____ sensation.

7. A standard ISO wine tasting glass is intended to hold up to _____ ounces.

8. The taste sensation of _____ is often the longest-lasting taste sensation, and is often the last taste to fade.

9. Wines are often tasted in related groups, known as _____.

10. Some unfiltered or unfined wines may appear cloudy or _____ by design.

11. The size and persistence of the bubbles in a sparkling wine is sometimes referred to as the _____.

12. If there are _____ present in a wine, they will most likely be detected using a "quick sniff" before swirling the glass.

13. A wine's _____ aromas should reveal any recognizable grape varieties, while the _____ aromas should reveal winemaking techniques such as the use of oak.

14. The term _____ is often used to indicate the scent of an aged wine.

15. The umami taste is somewhat rare in wine, but it may be detected in wines that have undergone _____ long enough for the yeast cells to decompose.

While there is no set standard and many "correct" ways to describe wine, a tasting note should clearly communicate the basic characteristics of a given wine, and—when used to describe wines to customers— should include the information that the customer wants to hear without intimidating or confusing them.

Consider, for example, the following tasting note: "Captain's Winery Monterey County Chardonnay 2015 is a yellow-hued white wine with brilliant clarity. The aromas include green apple, lemon, peach, vanilla, and smoke. It is medium-bodied and dry, with a high level of acidity, medium alcohol, and flavors of peach, green apple, and spice. This is a well-balanced, excellent quality wine with a long finish." Tasting notes such as this can be created using a template—such as the one that follows—as a starting point:

Table 21-1: Suggested Template for a Wine Tasting Note—Example

Characteristic:	Suggested terminology:	Example:
Name of the wine	Include (as applicable) the name of the producer, the type of the wine, the region of origin, and the vintage date	*Captain's Winery Monterey County Chardonnay 2015*
Type	White, Rosé, Red, Fortified, Sparkling	*This is a yellow-hued white wine with brilliant clarity*
Color	White: Yellow/Green, Yellow, Gold Rosé: Pink, Salmon, Orange Red: Purple, Ruby, Garnet, Tawny, Amber, Brown	
Clarity	Dull – Clear - Brilliant	
Aromas	See Appendix D (Wine Aroma Checklist) for possible terminology	*The aromas include green apple, lemon, peach, vanilla, and smoke.*
Sweetness	Dry – Off-dry – Sweet	*This wine is medium-bodied and dry, with a high level of acidity and medium alcohol. The wine has no tannin and no discernible bitterness.*
Acidity	Low – Medium - High	
Bitterness	None – Low – Medium – High	
Tannin	None – Low – Medium – High	
Alcohol	Low – Medium – High	
Body	Light – Medium – Full	
Flavors	See Appendix D (Wine Aroma Checklist) for possible terminology	*The flavors include peach, green apple, and cinnamon.*
Finish	Short – Medium - Long	*The wine has a long finish.*
Other characteristics	Balance, complexity, intensity, or others	*This is a well-balanced, highly complex, and intensely aromatic wine.*
Quality	Poor – Acceptable – Good – Very Good – Excellent	*This is an excellent quality wine.*

Table 21-2: Blank Template for a Wine Tasting Note

Characteristic:	Suggested terminology:	Example:
Name of the wine	Include (as applicable) the name of the producer, the type of the wine, the region of origin, and the vintage date	
Type	White, Rosé, Red, Fortified, Sparkling	
Color	White: Yellow/Green, Yellow, Gold Rosé: Pink, Salmon, Orange Red: Purple, Ruby, Garnet, Tawny, Amber, Brown	
Clarity	Dull – Clear - Brilliant	
Aromas	See Appendix D (Wine Aroma Checklist) for possible terminology	
Sweetness	Dry – Off-dry – Sweet	
Acidity	Low – Medium - High	
Bitterness	None – Low – Medium – High	
Tannin	None – Low – Medium – High	
Alcohol	Low – Medium – High	
Body	Light – Medium – Full	
Flavors	See Appendix D (Wine Aroma Checklist) for possible terminology	
Finish	Short – Medium - Long	
Other characteristics	Balance, complexity, intensity, or others	
Quality	Poor – Acceptable – Good – Very Good – Excellent	

1. On average, a taster will be able to recognize sweetness in a wine if it contains at least _____ residual sugar.
   a. 0.05%
   b. 1%
   c. 2%
   d. 3%

2. Humans are most sensitive to which of the following taste components?
   a. Bitterness
   b. Sweetness
   c. Acidity
   d. Fruitiness

3. Humans are least sensitive to which of the following taste components?
   a. Bitterness
   b. Sweetness
   c. Acidity
   d. Fruitiness

4. Yellow-green hues are most likely to be found in which of the following types of wine?
   a. Older white wines
   b. Young white wines from warm growing regions
   c. White wines that have been barrel-aged
   d. Young white wines from cool growing regions

5. Ruby-orange highlights are most likely to be found in which of the following styles of wine?
   a. Low-acid reds
   b. High-acid whites
   c. High-acid reds
   d. Low-acid whites

6. A turbid appearance is most likely to be found in which of the following styles of wine?
   a. Sparkling wine
   b. Unfiltered wine
   c. Blended wine
   d. High-acid wine

7. Which of the following substances can produce up to three sensory sensations, including a hot tactile sensation, a sweet taste, and a pungent odor?
   a. Tannin
   b. Residual sugar
   c. Alcohol
   d. Tartaric acid

8. Which of the following styles of wine is most likely to be described as astringent?
   a. Mature red Bordeaux
   b. Young Napa Cabernet Sauvignon
   c. Aged white Burgundy
   d. Sauternes

9. Manzanilla Sherry often displays this taste component, which is otherwise somewhat rare in wine:
   a. Saltiness
   b. Sweetness
   c. Acidity
   d. Astringency

10. Which of the following is the source of the umami taste component?
    a. Carbohydrates
    b. Ascorbic acid
    c. Sodium chloride
    d. Amino acids

THE IMPACT OF ALCOHOL ON HEALTH

CHAPTER TWENTY-TWO

LEARNING OBJECTIVES

After studying this chapter, the candidate should be able to:

- Recognize the potential negative consequences of excessive alcohol consumption.
- Discuss the potential health benefits of the moderate intake of alcohol.
- Recall what resveratrol is and how it impacts one's health.
- Understand how to achieve a healthy balance between the risks and benefits associated with alcohol consumption.

EXERCISE 1: THE IMPACT OF ALCOHOL ON HEALTH: FILL IN THE BLANK/SHORT ANSWER

Fill in the blanks for the following statements or questions.

1. _____, the by-product produced when alcohol is metabolized
   in the liver, can build up in the bloodstream and cause_____.

2. _____, defined as consuming large amounts of alcohol one or two nights
   a week, is one of the leading causes of death among young people.

3. The USDA recommends _____ drink per day for women, and
   _____ drinks per day for men, as a definition of "moderate consumption."

4. The definition of "one serving" of wine (at 12% to 14% abv) is _____.

5. The definition of "one serving" of beer (at 5% abv) is _____.

6. The definition of "one serving" of spirits (at 40% abv) is _____.

7. Some studies have shown that a decreased risk of coronary heart disease correlates with moderate drinking,
   most likely due to the _____ and _____-reducing effects of alcohol.

8. It is important to remember that alcohol _____ blood pressure.

9. Excessive amounts of alcohol can lead to _____, a condition where fat
   accumulates within the cells of the liver.

10. _____ is a nonreversible liver condition that can result from excessive
    alcohol consumption.

11. _____ is a beneficial phenolic compound found in red wine that has been
    shown to have anti-aging and disease-fighting properties.

1. Which of the following is considered to be a generally safe level of "moderate drinking," as defined by the USDA?
   a. Up to one drink a day for both men and women
   b. Up to two drinks a day for both men and women
   c. Up to one drink a day for women, and up to two drinks a day for men
   d. Up to one drink a day for men, and up to two drinks per day for women

2. Which of the following is considered to be "one serving" of wine (at 12% to 14% abv), as defined by the USDA?
   a. 4 ounces (118 ml)
   b. 5 ounces (148 ml)
   c. 8 ounces (237 ml)
   d. 10 ounces (296 ml)

3. Which of the following is considered to be "one serving" of beer (at 5% abv), as defined by the USDA?
   a. 12 ounces (355 ml)
   b. 14 ounces (414 ml)
   c. 16 ounces (473 ml)
   d. 20 ounces (591 ml)

4. Which of the following is considered to be "one serving" of spirits (at 40% abv), as defined by the USDA?
   a. ¾ ounce (22 ml)
   b. 1 ounce (30 ml)
   c. 1½ ounces (44 ml)
   d. 2 ounces (59 ml)

5. Which of the following is a beneficial compound often found in red wine and known to have anti-aging and disease-fighting properties?
   a. Flavonols
   b. Acetaldehyde
   c. Methanol
   d. Resveratrol

WINE ETIQUETTE AND SERVICE

CHAPTER TWENTY-THREE

LEARNING OBJECTIVES

After studying this chapter, the candidate should be able to:

- Describe the factors involved in professional wine service, including setup, glassware, opening a bottle, and order of service.
- Understand how temperature, decanting, and storage impact the perceived qualities of a wine.

- Recall the elements of best practices in food and wine pairing.
- Recognize how fat, salt, sweetness, acidity, and bitterness in foods impact the flavors of wine.
- Describe the key actions wine professionals can take to ensure the responsible service of alcohol.

EXERCISE 1: WINE SERVICE: TRUE OR FALSE

Mark each of the following statements as true or false.

1. _____ On a restaurant table, wine glasses should be set to the left of the water glasses.

2. _____ If you need to set glasses while the customer is seated, it is best to place the glasses on the table from the right-hand side of the customer.

3. _____ Soap residue left on flutes will cause the bubbles in a sparkling wine to become agitated and will often cause the glass to overflow.

4. _____ A combination of ice and water will chill wine faster than ice alone.

5. _____ Some people prefer high-acid reds, such as Chianti and Beaujolais, to be served slightly chilled.

6. _____ A bottle of wine that has been ordered by the host should be presented to him or her before opening, with the label facing up.

7. _____ After removing the top of the capsule from a bottle of wine, it should be placed on the table or in the ice bucket.

8. _____ Once removed from the bottle, the cork should be placed on the table, to the right of the host.

9. _____ While pouring wine at a restaurant table, it is customary to move clockwise around the table.

10. _____ Upon approval of the wine, the host should always be served first, regardless of gender.

11. _____ Using a 5-ounce pour, one standard bottle of wine should easily serve 7 people.

Fill in the blanks or give a short answer for the following statements or questions.

1. When removing the cork from a bottle of sparkling wine, it is advisable to hold the bottle at a _____ degree angle.

2. Let loose, a Champagne cork can fly across the room at _____ mph.

3. Sparkling wines should be served at a temperature of _____.

4. If red wine is served too warm, the taste of _____ may become predominant.

5. The purpose of decanting is to allow a wine's _____ and _____ to develop by exposing it to oxygen.

6. _____ wines may be improved via decanting to soften and mellow out their tannins with exposure to air.

7. Complex wines with _____ aging may be improved by being decanted an hour or two before serving, as this may allow their _____ to open and expand.

8. _____ should be decanted with care and consumed immediately after decanting.

9. Wines with _____ in the bottle should be placed upright for an hour or so before service.

10. _____ white wines such as those produced by Domaine Zind-Humbrecht may improve with decanting to reduce their reductive nature.

11. What is the ideal temperature for a wine cellar?_____

12. What is the ideal level of humidity for a wine cellar? _____

13. Ideal wine storage conditions include storage for the bottles on their side, so that the _____ does not dry out.

EXERCISE 3: FOOD AND WINE PAIRING/FILL IN THE BLANK

Using the term "increases" or "decreases," fill in the blanks in each of the following statements in order to state how a specific food component is expected to impact the perceived flavor of a wine.

The Interaction of Wine and Food	
Food Component:	**Expected impact on wine: Increases or decreases**
Acidity	_____ the perceived acidity of a wine
	_____ the perceived sweetness of a wine
	_____ the perceived body (richness) of a wine
Sweetness	_____ the perceived acidity of a wine
	_____ the perceived sweetness of a wine
	_____ the perceived fruitiness of a wine
	_____ the perceived body (richness) of a wine
	_____ perceived "heat" from spicy food
Saltiness	_____ the perceived fruitiness of a wine
	_____ the perceived body (richness) of a wine
	_____ the perceived bitterness of a wine
Bitterness	_____ the perceived bitterness of a wine
Umami	_____ the perceived sweetness of a wine
	_____ the perceived fruitiness of a wine
	_____ the perceived body (richness) of a wine
	_____ the perceived bitterness of a wine

1. Which of the following practices will chill a bottle of wine the fastest?
   a. Placing the bottle in the bottom of the refrigerator
   b. Placing the bottle in the top of the refrigerator
   c. Placing the bottle on ice
   d. Placing the bottle in a combination of ice and cold water

2. Which of the following is the best practice to follow for the table service of wine?
   a. Serve from the customer's left, with the wine glass placed on the left-hand side of the customer's place setting.
   b. Serve from the customer's left, with the wine glass placed on the right-hand side of the customer's place setting.
   c. Serve from the customer's right, with the wine glass placed on the right-hand side of the customer's place setting.
   d. Serve from the customer's right, with the wine glass placed on the left-hand side of the customer's place setting.

3. How many standard 5-ounce pours does a standard 750-ml bottle contain?
   a. Four
   b. Five
   c. Six
   d. Seven

4. Of the following wines, which should be served the coldest?
   a. Dry white Bordeaux
   b. Oregon Pinot Noir
   c. Nonvintage Champagne
   d. Beaujolais Nouveau

5. Of the following wines, which should be served the warmest?
   a. Full-bodied red wines
   b. Light-bodied red wines
   c. Sweet white wines
   d. Full-bodied white wines

6. Which of the following wines may be suitable for decanting?
   a. Young, robust reds
   b. Complex wines with moderate aging
   c. Fully aged, mature red wines
   d. All of the above

7. What are the ideal conditions for a wine cellar?
   a. Cool temperatures between 50°F and 60°F (10°C and 15°C), and humidity of 65–75%
   b. Cool temperatures between 60°F and 70°F (15°C and 21°C), and humidity of 65–75%
   c. Cool temperatures between 50°F and 60°F (10°C and 15°C), and humidity of 30–40%
   d. Cool temperatures between 60°F and 70°F (15°C and 21°C), and humidity of 30–40%

8. During table service, what is the appropriate thing to do once the server has removed the capsule from the top of the wine bottle?
   a. The server should present it to the host.
   b. The server should place it on the table.
   c. The server should place it in an apron or pocket.
   d. The server should place it in an ice bucket.

9. During table service, what is the appropriate thing to do once the server has removed the cork from the bottle?
   a. The server should place it in an apron or pocket.
   b. The server should place it on the table to the right of the host.
   c. The server should hand it to the host.
   d. The server should quickly sniff the cork to see if TCA can be detected.

10. Which of the following practices is advised when opening sparkling wine?
    a. Remove the capsule and the cage before attempting to remove the cork.
    b. Keep the bottle in an ice bucket while removing the cage.
    c. Remove the cork before you chill the bottle.
    d. Hold the bottle at a 45° angle and keep a good grip on the cork.

ADDITIONAL MATERIALS: BLANK WINE MAPS

Figure A-1: Blank Wine Map of Bordeaux

Figure A-2: Blank Wine Map of the Loire Valley

Figure A-3: Blank Wine Map of the Côte de Nuits

Figure A-4: Blank Wine Map of the Côte de Beaune

Figure A-5: Blank Wine Map of Beaujolais

Figure A-6: Blank Wine Map of the Rhône Valley

Figure A-7: Blank Wine Map of the Languedoc-Roussillon

Figure A-8: Blank Wine Map of Italy

Figure A-9: Blank Wine Map of Veneto

Figure A-10: Blank Wine Map of Piedmont

Figure A-11: Blank Wine Map of Tuscany

Figure A-12: Blank Wine Map of Spain

Figure A-13: Blank Wine Map of Portugal

Figure A-14: Blank Wine Map of Germany

Figure A-15: Blank Wine Map of Austria

Figure A-16: Blank Wine Map of Napa County

Copyright: The Society of Wine Educators

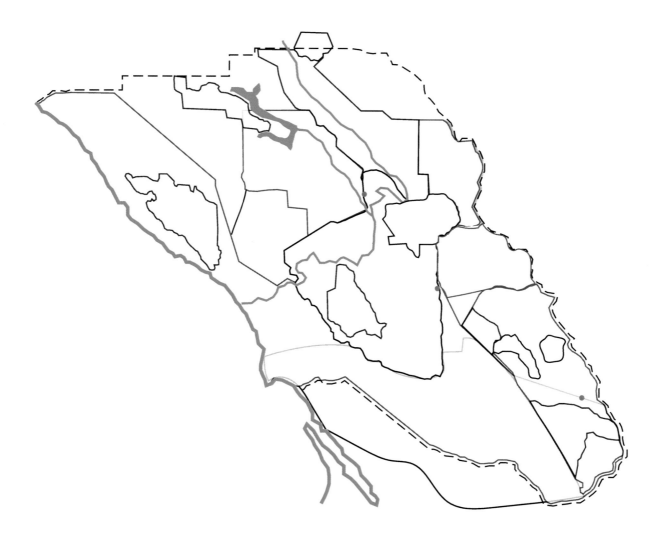

Figure A-17: Blank Wine Map of Sonoma County

Figure A-18: Blank Wine Map of California's Central Coast

Figure A-19: Blank Wine Map of Washington State

Figure A-20: Blank Wine Map of Oregon

Figure A-21: Blank Wine Map of the Willamette Valley

Figure A-22: Blank Wine Map of Argentina

Figure A-23: Blank Wine Map of Chile

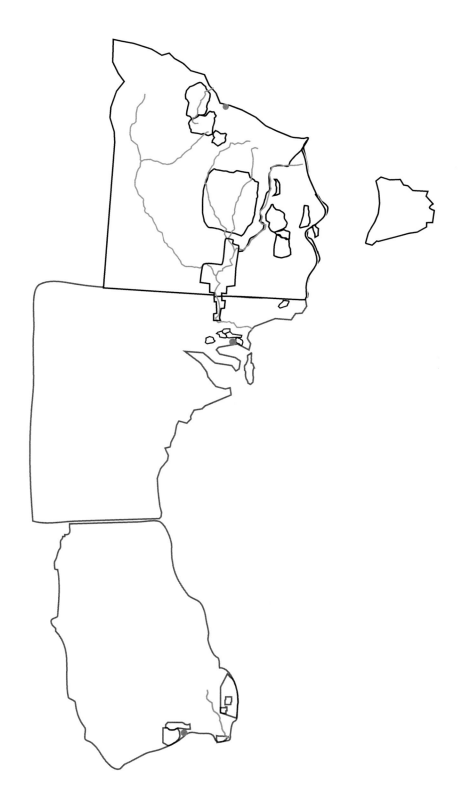

Figure A-24: Blank Wine Map of Australia

Figure A-25: Blank Wine Map of New Zealand

Figure A-26: Blank Wine Map of South Africa